UMAMI

UMAMI UMAMI

UMAMI

うまみ

# FLAVOR BOMBS

## The Umami Ingredients That Make Taste Explode

### ADAM FLEISCHMAN

with Tien Nguyen

*Photographs by* Wendy Sue Lamm

A Rux Martin Book
Houghton Mifflin Harcourt
Boston New York 2018

For information about permission to reproduce selections from
this book, write to trade.permissions@hmhco.com or to Permissions,
Houghton Mifflin Harcourt Publishing Company, 3 Park Avenue,
19th Floor, New York, New York 10016.

hmhco.com

Library of Congress Cataloging-in-Publication Data
Names: Fleischman, Adam, author. | Nguyen, Tien (Tien Z.), author. | Lamm,
Wendy Sue, photographer.
Title: Flavor bombs : the umami ingredients that make taste explode / Adam
Fleischman with Tien Nguyen ; photographs by Wendy Sue Lamm.
Description: Boston : Houghton Mifflin Harcourt, 2018. | "A Rux Martin book."
| Includes index.
Identifiers: LCCN 2017051896 (print) | LCCN 2018000946 (ebook) | ISBN
9780544784901 (ebook) | ISBN 9780544784895 (hardback)
Subjects: LCSH: Condiments | Cooking (Spices) | Food—Composition. | Umami
(Taste) | BISAC: COOKING / General. | LCGFT: Cookbooks.
Classification: LCC TX819.A1 (ebook) | LCC TX819.A1 F55 2018 (print)
LC record available at https://lccn.loc.gov/2017051896

Book design by Raphael Geroni
Food and prop styling by Adam Fleischman

Printed in China

C&C 10 9 8 7 6 5 4 3 2 1

To those for whom food is their escape,
and perhaps their homecoming

# ACKNOWLEDGMENTS

Thanks to Marc Gerald at United Talent Agency, for pushing me to expand my horizons and do this fun project. To Tien Nguyen, for her skill and patience. To Wendy Sue Lamm, for her vision and collaborative perfection.

To my family, Theo and Pelle, for their constant inspiration and curiosity, and everyone who inspires me in the kitchens I visit and have worked in over the years.

# CONTENTS

# Introduction

**'M NOT THE LIKELIEST GUY** to have built a world around *umami*. Far from it, actually.

I taught myself how to cook mostly by screwing up. I didn't (and still don't) have much patience to read a recipe or a cookbook in detail and follow the directions step by step. Instead I have a little bit of a beginner's mind-set when I pick up a recipe. Take, for example, a recipe for meatloaf. I look at it as if I've never seen a recipe for meatloaf before, absorb its nuances, and then I forget most of the details after I turn away from the book. Once I start cooking and making mistakes, that's when I start learning.

I started cooking because I love to eat. I went from eating out at all the restaurants in town to devouring all the cookbooks I could get my hands on to re-create the magic in my own kitchen.

Heston Blumenthal, the chef and owner of The Fat Duck in Berkshire, England, had a huge influence on the way I cook. I watched his shows religiously, especially *In Search of Perfection*, where he would deconstruct classic recipes to learn how they worked, then reconstruct and refine them. He had a perfectionist streak that I related to.

Blumenthal was also critical for something else: He introduced me to umami in the mid-2000s. The discovery of umami goes back way farther than that, to 1908, when a Japanese scientist named Kikunae Ikeda put a name to the savory, meaty flavor that gives foods like cheeses and mushrooms their extra oomph. At The Fat Duck, Blumenthal took umami-rich ingredients and put his spins on them.

Despite all the newfangled, fancy chef-y things that were happening with umami, it was the simple burger that brought its importance home to me. I was at In-N-Out Burger, one of the best—if not *the* best—classic American burger chains in L.A., when it hit me: Deconstruct a burger and what do you get? A nicely seared patty, melted cheese, caramelized onions, tomatoes, ketchup. These are all umami ingredients, I realized, stacked one right on top of another and stuck between two buns.

I considered another super-popular food that Americans love: pizza. Pizza also is packed with umami ingredients. At the most basic level, after all, most pizzas are rich tomato sauce plus melted mozzarella cheese, both high in umami. Throw on a topping like mushrooms or sausage and you have even more umami.

It's absolutely no coincidence that burgers and pizzas are such popular, beloved American foods. They are umami bombs. What people crave isn't a burger or a pizza. What people crave is *within* the burger or the pizza: the seared meat, the cheese, the tomato sauce. What we crave is umami. The burger bun and pizza crust essentially function as neutral carb bases for convenient flavor delivery.

Once I realized this, I knew I wanted to create a restaurant that delivered umami bombs in every bite. It would deeply satisfy and inspire cravings at the same time. I liked the idea of juxtaposing something conceptual and sophisticated with something commonplace. If I could sell a burger or a pizza with high-quality ingredients for, say, $10, something super flavorful, something full of umami, I might be able to make the idea work, especially in a town like L.A.

# BRINGING UMAMI HOME

TO ROUND UP INGREDIENTS RICH IN UMAMI, I WENT TO MIT-suwa, a Japanese grocery in West L.A., and threw anything and everything that looked savory into my basket. Bottles of light and dark soy sauce, bottles of fish sauce, bottles of Maggi Liquid Seasoning. Bags of dried fish heads and dried mushrooms. Little jars of seaweed powder, a jar of bonito flakes. Packets of dashi (the base for Japanese broth), squat containers of miso. (All these things are available in Asian markets, some supermarkets, and online. In Sources, page 248, I tell you where to find them.)

This wasn't going to be a traditional burger. Most burgers, like the ones you eat at Shake Shack and In-N-Out, are nostalgic, old-fashioned, retro. Which is great and delicious, but I didn't want to be looking back at the past. I wanted to be creating the future, with modern techniques and global influences.

With my mind set on what I wanted, I began to experiment with flavor combinations, with sauces, with the bun-to-patty ratio. As an homage to Heston Blumenthal, an Englishman through and through, I created a Port and Stilton Burger with high-quality beef that I gently massaged into a patty.

That was the birth of the original Umami Burger. I knew I had a blockbuster. I had $40,000 in my savings account, and I put it all into a small restaurant on La Brea Avenue in the middle of Los Angeles. But my pursuit of flavor was just starting to take off.

# WHEREFORE ART THOU, UMAMI?

**N**OT ALL FOOD HAS UMAMI, BUT A LOT OF GREAT FOOD DOES: Italian dishes, veal stock reductions, and of course, Japanese cuisine. Japanese dishes are filled with umami-rich ingredients, like dashi, bonito flakes, and soy sauce.

Dr. Kikunae Ikeda discovered umami when he was a professor at what was then Tokyo Imperial University (now the University of Tokyo). As it turns out, Ikeda was a food guy. The story goes that over a fantastic bowl of dashi, he began wondering why his soup had a distinctly savory, meaty flavor even though it didn't have any meat in it. It was the same flavor, he would later say in one of his lectures, that was common to tomatoes, cheeses, asparagus, and meats. It wasn't quite salty, or sweet, or bitter, or sour. It was something else entirely.

He made a huge pot of dashi and set out to investigate what that something else was. It helped that dashi has only two primary components: dried seaweed (*kombu*) and bonito flakes. He analyzed the kombu and found it contained powerful amounts of an amino acid—glutamate—that he was able to link to that distinct savory taste. He called it *umami*, which roughly translates to "tasty," or "delicious."

Not too long after Dr. Ikeda made this discovery, Japanese researchers also discovered molecules in food that have umami properties. Specifically, the nucleotides inosine monophosphate (found in bonito flakes) and guanosine monophosphate (mostly in mushrooms) were shown to help carry the savory flavor of umami and amplify savoriness of food when combined with foods high in glutamates. And in the past few decades, researchers in the field have found still other nucleotides that, like inosinate and guanylate, trigger the irreplaceable taste of umami.

In retrospect it's not too surprising that Dr. Ikeda had his moment of inspiration over a bowl of dashi: Kombu is one of the most umami-rich ingredients out there. We all have tasted umami since birth. Glutamate makes up roughly half of the amino acids in mothers' milk, and a lot of what we eat every day has umami in it. In 2001, almost 100 years after Dr. Ikeda made his discovery, scientists confirmed there are receptors on your tongue that specifically taste these umami flavors.

Umami flavors are *everywhere*, not just in Japanese food. You can taste umami in raw foods like egg yolks and super ripe tomatoes picked right off the vine. Other foods, like beef, cheese, and Chinese cabbage, benefit from cooking, aging, or fermenting to unleash their umami properties. You'll find umami in the Parmigiano-Reggiano and marinara sauce at your favorite Italian restaurant. You'll find it in the kimchi at your local Korean BBQ joint. In the taco shop, it's in the Cotija cheese and the salsa verde made with roasted tomatillos. And there it is in the fish sauce in the rice noodle salad at your favorite Vietnamese restaurant.

While all of these singular ingredients have a strong element of umami on their own, they have an exponentially bigger impact when combined. Dashi with kombu is ok; dashi with kombu and bonito flakes is even better. A pasta sauce made with ripe tomatoes is good; a pasta sauce made with ripe tomatoes and spiked with a little bit of anchovy—way better. And a classic cheeseburger, like the one you get at In-N-Out? It's so craveable in part because of a formidable umami combo: ketchup, cheese, caramelized onions, tomatoes.

### GLUTAMATE-RICH INGREDIENTS

| PROTEIN | PRODUCE | CHEESE | SEASONINGS | PANTRY |
|---|---|---|---|---|
| Anchovies | Broccoli | Cheddar | Fish sauce | Dried shiitake mushrooms |
| Beef | Carrots | Emmenthal | Ketchup | Kombu |
| Chicken | Chinese cabbage | Gorgonzola | Marmite | Nori |
| Clams | Corn | Gruyère | Miso | Star anise |
| Crab | Green peas | Parmesan | Soy sauce | Walnuts |
| Cured ham, like prosciutto | Lentils | Raclette | Worcestershire sauce | |
| Duck | Onions | Ricotta | | |
| Oysters | Potatoes | Roquefort | | |
| Pork | Ripe tomatoes | Stilton | | |
| Scallops | Shiitake mushrooms | | | |
| Sea urchin (uni) | Soybeans | | | |
| Shrimp and prawns | Spinach | | | |
| Squid | Strawberries | | | |
| Veal | Sun-dried tomatoes | | | |
| | Sweet potatoes | | | |
| | Truffles | | | |

| INOSINATE-RICH INGREDIENTS | GUANYLATE-RICH INGREDIENTS |
|---|---|
| Beef | Dried morel mushrooms |
| Chicken | Dried oyster mushrooms |
| Cod | Dried porcini mushrooms |
| Dried bonito flakes | Dried shiitake mushrooms |
| Dried sardines | Matsutake mushrooms |
| Fresh sardines | Nori |
| Mackerel | Truffles |
| Pork | |
| Shrimp | |
| Snow crab | |
| Truffles | |
| Tuna | |

# UMAMI SYNERGY

**A**LL OF THE INGREDIENTS ON THE OPPOSITE PAGE ARE TASTY on their own, but mix a glutamate-rich ingredient with one rich in inosinate or guanylate and you'll find that the flavor amplifies exponentially. That's what scientists call umami synergy, and it's prevalent in a bunch of classic dishes. Indeed, if there's a dish that you love and go back to time and time again, chances are it contains multiple umami ingredients. The dashi that caught Ikeda's attention, for example, is so simple yet so satisfying because its two key components, kombu and bonito flakes, are umami ingredients that work together. Other examples of classic umami combinations:

Tomato sauce + Parmesan cheese

Hamburger + Cheddar cheese

Mirepoix (diced onion, celery, and carrot with aromatic herbs) + Beef stock

Dashi + Miso

Chicken stock + Chinese cabbage

Of course you can't just throw all the umami ingredients together in a dish and expect a flavor explosion. Umami, after all, is different than just rich; it's a bowl of ramen with flavors that are balanced rather than one pounding note. The wise cook knows how to capitalize on this synergy and combines the right ingredients in the right amounts in the right way to make a delicious dish. That's putting the art in the science, and with a little practice, you'll be the wise cook in no time.

# TECHNIQUES TO AMPLIFY UMAMI

WITH A LITTLE PRACTICE, YOU CAN BRING OUT EXTRA punches of umami flavor with simple cooking techniques.

### SEARING

Properly searing is one of the most important techniques in cooking, period. You have to sear over high heat because it's the high heat that activates a chemical domino effect called the Maillard reaction, where amino acids and simple sugars in an ingredient react, browning and, crucially, creating hundreds of flavor compounds. That reaction is what makes a nicely seared steak or roasted tomatoes taste so delicious.

### SALTING

Salt is not only a crucial seasoning for most dishes, it also brings out and enhances the other flavors of your dish. Most people tend to undersalt; if you're apprehensive, start with a little bit and keep adding until you think you're at the edge of oversalting. Experiment a bit. You might be surprised how that extra pinch transforms the entire dish.

### TIME

Long cooking is often the key to greatness. A sauce that's good today will be even better tomorrow, after the flavors have time to really meld and integrate. Fermenting, aging, and curing are all techniques that rely on time to develop flavor. When wine is stored away to age for a few months or years or even decades, or when cabbage is put in salt solution to ferment for weeks to make kimchi, it's time that allows the enzymes and microbes to break everything down. The result is a deep, complex, sometimes even funky flavor.

Umami + Time = Flavor.

# CHAOS IN THE KITCHEN: BEYOND RECIPES

## ADAM'S PRINCIPLES OF FLAVOR

1. Your palate has a memory of flavors. Use it.
2. Start with a clear concept of what you are cooking.
3. The more you hate a dish, the more likely it is that you'll come to love it later.
4. Taste is malleable depending on context.
5. The expectations you have before you take one bite strongly influence how that dish will taste. Be clear on your concept.
6. Chaos can inspire great dishes.
7. Deliciousness is messy at first.
8. Balance is key.
9. Cook without fear.
10. All meals need some umami.

ONCE I GOT A HANDLE ON UMAMIFYING BURGERS AND PIZZA, I started integrating fish sauce, soy sauce, and dried mushrooms into my sauces to see what would happen. I love chocolate—in fact I consider it an honorary umami ingredient because it's satisfying in the same way umami ingredients are—so even though it may sound a little strange, I took a chance and threw some truffles in with melted chocolate to see if their flavors were complementary. Surprise: The pairing works! (See page 232.)

Of course it took a fair amount of trial and error before I had recipes that I could commit to paper and share with my friends. Along the way, I made a ton of mistakes: I didn't put enough acid in a dressing. I added more fish sauce to a pasta sauce than I should have. I didn't cook onions long enough to let them truly caramelize and develop flavor. I don't regret any one of these mistakes. In fact the mistakes are crucial.

Cooking involves gleaning lessons from failures and surprises. Back when I was teaching myself how to cook by obsessively making the same dish over and over again, I once used 99-percent-fat-free turkey instead of a fatty mix of ground pork and beef to make meatloaf. I learned from the bone-dry result that fat equals moisture. That's a fundamental lesson in cooking meats. I've made a lot of meatloaf since then, but I'm still no master of it. I don't want to be. If I think I am, I know I'll settle in my ways instead of striving to make a better meatloaf the next time.

The recipes in this book are the capturing of dishes that were made after the basics were mastered. But you have the final say. This book is here to give you recipes, definitely, but also to give you the tools to bring out umami in your own dishes by incorporating those flavors and mastering those cooking techniques. And if you don't have the courage already, I hope this book gives you enough to get out of your head and just start cooking.

Read through the recipes, but don't feel tied to them. Don't overthink the process. Don't sweat about re-creating the photographs. *Do* be patient: You can't rush great food. It needs to blossom and coalesce. And when you allow the flavors to develop, you'll never catch the dreaded bland-food curse.

And with every step, with every mistake, with every success, you're learning something much more important than how to make pretty food. You're learning the foundations of cooking.

What if you don't have everything that a recipe calls for? Don't procrastinate because you don't think you're ready. You are ready. Do it anyway. You can always make it differently next time, when you do have everything you need. In my experience the best lessons always happen when you are badly prepared, not ready, or can use one more thing. Why? Because that's when you try harder, and that creative power enters the dish. In cooking as in any art, deprivation breeds inspiration—maybe more so in cooking because our core sustenance is tied to it. Have less and you will create more. Think of the hundreds of things cooks have found to do with flour. With an egg. Show me a state-of-the-art kitchen, and I will show you some uninspired food. Show me a table with a pan on it next to a fire, and I will show you the possibility for great food.

We all have a little bit of fear when approaching the stove, and that's natural. But trust that a moment of truth will always occur when you get there. Seize the fear. Quell it. Cook.

And after the mistakes have been made and you do cook that dish perfectly, there is true beauty in knowing that when that perfection is achieved, it will not show itself in that exact way again. The dish will be eaten just once, and it'll never taste exactly the same. That's cooking.

Amateurs built the Ark; professionals, the *Titanic*. And amateurs can create magic in the kitchen. The spontaneous creations from a cook's heart often trump the most practiced recipes of a culinary master. You can do it. Let chaos reign.

# The Basic Pantry

**I USE ORGANIC PRODUCTS WHENEVER POSSIBLE.**

### DRIED BEANS

Pintos, garbanzos, gigantes . . . you can never have too many dried beans in your pantry. Legumes are healthy, easy-to-make pantry staples that are great foils for soaking up umami flavors. I prefer Rancho Gordo brand, as they produce a rainbow of artisanal beans. (See Sources, page 248.)

### HERBS

Always use fresh herbs. I can't think of one dried herb that's better than the fresh version.

### NOODLES

Keep dried pasta on hand. Always. It's high quality, low effort. My favorite brand of Italian pasta is Rustichella d'Abruzzo, which you can find on Amazon. In addition to pasta, I keep my pantry stocked with other dried noodles, like ramen noodles, egg noodles, and rice noodles.

### OLIVE OIL

Just like I do with salts, I keep a variety of olive oils in the pantry. For a good all-purpose, everyday option, a mild, buttery Arbequina olive oil is great. If you can afford it, spend on a really nice extra-virgin olive oil for special occasions or when the olive oil in a dish will really shine, like when it's the final touch on a dish and the first thing you'll taste when you take a bite.

### PEPPADEW PEPPERS

Peppadews are pickled red piquante peppers from South Africa. About the size of cherry tomatoes, they're sweet, spicy, and a little tangy. They're sold in jars, and even the liquid that they're packed in has a nice zip.

### PEPPER

Freshly ground black pepper is a must. White pepper is milder and nice to have for light, delicate sauces.

### SALT

I keep a couple different salts on hand for various purposes. For everyday cooking I prefer the taste of sea salt. If I'm heavily salting something like fish, or brining, I use kosher salt because of its ubiquity and affordability. And a nice fleur de sel is always great for that last-second flourish on a dish before serving.

The Umami Pantry

# The Umami Pantry

THERE ARE MANY, MANY INGREDIENTS THAT HAVE A LOT OF natural umami in them. Of course, I keep a lot of them in my pantry and fridge. These umami ingredients—along with basic seasonings like acid, salt, and heat—are added in intervals, always at least at the beginning, middle, and end.

Mix this umami pantry with some cherished memories of meals past, a little risk taking, and patience, and you will be a great cook in no time.

## ANCHOVY FILLETS, ANCHOVY PASTE, and DRIED ANCHOVIES

Anchovies pack a ton of umami, and they meld into sauces perfectly. The fillets come in cans that are easy to store in the pantry, but the tubes of paste are good for those times you just need a hint of umami and don't want to break open a new tin of fillets. Two fillets are equal to about 1 teaspoon of paste. I also have a packet or two of dried anchovies in my pantry, which you can pick up at an Asian grocery store or online at Amazon. Once you open a pack, place it in an airtight container or bag and toss it in the fridge if you'll use the rest within a week. For longer storage, it'll keep better in the freezer.

## CANNED ITALIAN or CALIFORNIAN TOMATOES

Fresh tomatoes are great for fresh recipes, like my Blender Gazpacho (page 84). But for sauces, gravies, stews, ragus, or anything else that requires actually cooking the tomatoes, canned is usually better. Canned tomatoes are grown specifically for their concentrated flavor. They are usually smaller tomatoes, with thicker flesh—which is where all that umami is.

## CHOCOLATE

Ok, I'm cheating a little here. Chocolate isn't technically an umami ingredient. But it gives you such a deep sense of satisfaction. Keep at least one bar around the kitchen. Always go with a trusted producer of chocolate: I like the chocolates from Callebaut, Michel Cluizel, Valrhona, Guittard, and Scharffen Berger. If you can't find those, chocolates from Belgium or France are good ones, though check the label. If sugar is the main ingredient, you're better off staying away.

## DRIED MUSHROOMS

Keep packets of dried porcinis, dried morels, and dried shiitakes in your pantry and throw them in a stock, or blitz them for a spice blend. Use the best-quality mushrooms that you can afford; my favorite dried mushrooms come from Far West Fungi (see Sources, page 248). If you're tossing them straight into a sauce, it's a good idea to first rinse them off in cold water to remove any dirt or grit. If you need to rehydrate the mushrooms before using, warm some water in a small saucepan over low heat. Turn off the heat and add the dried mushrooms. Soak the mushrooms until they're completely rehydrated, 20 to 30 minutes, and then strain the water through a fine-mesh sieve or coffee filter; discard any grit or dirt. The mushrooms and their flavorful liquid will then be ready to go.

### DUCK FAT

Buy a container of duck fat and keep it in your freezer. You can often find duck fat at Whole Foods or your local specialty grocer; Amazon carries it as well. It's surprisingly useful: You can use it to confit, of course, or use it instead of olive oil or butter when sautéing vegetables or crisping potatoes. It'll add an inimitable depth of flavor.

### EGGS

The umami in eggs is found mostly in the yolks. For all my recipes, I use large, organic, pasture-raised eggs.

### FISH SAUCE

Fish sauce has a ton of umami in it. It won't necessarily make your food fishy; used in measured amounts, it'll actually bring out the meatiness of your food. Quality varies enormously, as does country of origin. My favorite bottle of fish sauce is the one made by Red Boat, a Vietnamese brand that offers both a nonkosher and kosher version.

### GREEN TEA and MATCHA

Green tea has high levels of theanine, an amino acid that is chemically very similar to glutamate and imparts a savory flavor similar to umami. Buy the highest quality you can afford. Matcha is a type of green tea that's been processed into a powder. It's often divided into two general categories: ceremonial grade and cooking (culinary) grade. Ceremonial-grade matcha has a natural sweetness, and that's what you use if you just want to brew the matcha to drink. Cooking-grade matcha is processed differently than ceremonial-grade matcha, as it's intended to be used as an ingredient and combined with other flavors. You can still brew it with hot water and drink it, but it won't be as sweet or delicate as the ceremonial-grade matcha.

### KOMBU

This dried seaweed is sold in rectangular sealed packages, usually at the Asian grocery store. It's crucial for making dashi, the Japanese broth. Keep it at room temp in your pantry; after opening, place it in a sealed bag and stash it back in your pantry. It'll last for a few months.

### MARMITE

Yeast has a ton of umami, and Marmite is basically that: It's a yeasty extract sold in distinctive squat jars at the supermarket. It's spread on toast and crackers and otherwise used as a condiment in the United Kingdom and Australia, but it's not nearly as popular here in the United States. It can take a while to acquire the taste if you're not used to it; to ease into it, try adding it to sauces. Once you open it, screw the lid back on tight and keep it on your counter or in your pantry. It'll last for years.

## MISO

Miso is a fermented paste made from soybeans. It comes in a wide range of colors, but the most common are white (*shiro*), yellow (*shishu*), and red (*aka*). Generally the lighter the miso, the milder the flavor. The darker misos have been fermented longer and so will have deeper, funkier flavors. Miso lasts forever in the fridge.

## PARMESAN CHEESE

Buy the best you can afford—Parmigiano-Reggiano is the best. Grate fresh with a Microplane, and use pre-grated only when it comes from a cheesemonger.

## PORK

Guanciale, pancetta, prosciutto, bacons, and salamis are all worth keeping around to add to other meats for a savory counterpoint.

## PRESERVED BLACK TRUFFLES

Truffles don't need to be pricey, or only used for special occasions. Good-quality preserved black truffles abound and are sold in slices, pastes, trimmings, and butters; you'll even find them pureed and packaged in tubes for ease of use. My friends at Truffle Brothers will ship you some (see Sources, page 248). Avoid using truffle oils (unless you make them yourself) because they often contain artificial scents and little flavor.

## SHIO KOJI

*Shio koji* is a creamy, fermented rice product that you can find at your local Japanese supermarket or online. Koji itself is a mold with high levels of enzymes that break down proteins and starches; give it some time to ferment with the right ingredients and you end up with soy sauce and miso paste and mirin and sake. I use shio koji to make sauces; it can also be used for marinades and dressings. After opening, store it in the fridge, where it'll last for about six months.

## SOY SAUCE, POWDERED SOY SAUCE, and TAMARI

I keep a few different soy sauce products in my pantry. I have a white soy sauce (which isn't white in color, though it is a lighter shade than most soys) for mellow flavor. I also keep a good all-purpose soy on hand, like the Japanese ones they sell at the Asian markets. I also keep a small pouch of powdered soy sauce handy, which is just the dry, dehydrated version of soy sauce, to use in my Master Dust (page 32). Tamari is similar to soy sauce, but thicker in texture and more complex in flavor.

## STOCK

Homemade stock is great, but if you don't have any on hand, don't let that stop you from making recipes that call for it. Instead, do what I do and keep packaged demi-glace that you can turn into stock in your pantry at all times. Savory Choice, for example, makes solid beef and chicken demi-glaces, which I use to make quick stocks by diluting them in water

(I start with equal parts demi-glace and water and adjust from there, depending on how intense I want the stock to be). Another idea: If you go out for ramen a lot, bring home the broth. Strain it and try using it in most any recipe that calls for stock.

### TOMATO PASTE

A tube of tomato paste in your cabinet will go a long way. Always get double-concentrated tomato paste.

### TRUFFLE HONEY

Another jar in your pantry that will last forever. Don't—I repeat, *do not*—buy any truffle honey that uses truffle oil. Instead look for truffle honey that really is made of real truffles and honey. Like truffle salt, truffle honey can be a little pricey, with a 4-ounce jar setting you back anywhere between $10 and $25, depending on where you get it. But also like truffle salt, a little bit goes a long way. It's worth the indulgence.

### TRUFFLE SALT

It is what it sounds like: salt infused with real truffle particulates. Pick out a good Italian or French one; if you can, smell before you buy, as the aroma will tell you everything about the quality of the jar. It may be a little expensive—between $10 and $15 for a 4-ounce jar or bag—but even a pinch is incredibly flavorful, so a small jar of truffle salt will last you a long while. If the salt stales over time—and it will—you can still use it: just use slightly more than what the recipe calls for.

### UMAMI MASTER SAUCE, UMAMI MASTER DUST, and UMAMI KETCHUP

These are all my own blends that I make in huge batches to deploy whenever I need them. See page 30.

### WORCESTERSHIRE SAUCE

Worcestershire sauce is fermented with a ton of umami ingredients, like anchovies and fish sauce. It's great not just on steaks but also in sauces and other things you want to amp up.

# UMAMI SIDEKICKS

**W**HEN COMBINED WITH UMAMI-RICH INGREDIENTS, THESE sidekicks hike up the flavor even more.

### A GREAT HOT SAUCE

Sriracha, Tabasco, pureed Calabrian chilies, *sambal oelek*. Choose your favorite. Spice things up.

### SHERRY WINE

Sherry wine comes from the southwestern part of Spain, and it's a fortified wine. I use dry (fino) sherry, mostly, throughout my cooking, as well as sweet sherries like Pedro Ximénez (P.X.).

### TOGARASHI

This is a spicy Japanese spice powder, usually sold in little bottles. The spices vary depending on the manufacturer, but they all contain several types of ground chilies and very often ground ginger, ground sesame seeds, and ground citrus peel. Just a shake or two on meat or in your bowl of noodle soup is all you need.

### VINEGARS

Vinegars are crucial to aciding things up. I use mostly top-quality sherry and balsamic vinegars.

### YUZU KOSHO

*Yuzu kosho* is a mixture of Japanese citrus (yuzu) and chile (kosho), and it's a condiment that I can't live without. It's very bright, so it's especially great with foods that are a little bland to start, like potatoes. There are two types: green and red. The green uses a green chile base; the red, a red chile base. Both are intense, and which one you use is a matter of taste. Keep the jars in the fridge, where they will last for several months.

# UMAMI MASTER RECIPES

**T**HESE THREE MASTER RECIPES ARE my go-tos for whenever I want to add a bit of extra oomph to whatever I'm cooking. You'll find them not only useful for the recipes in this book but also for your cooking in general. Make big batches of each and store them in your fridge or pantry.

*Highlighted ingredients are staples of the Umami Pantry (page 24).*

# UMAMI MASTER DUST

## MAKES 2 CUPS

THIS MASTER DUST IS SUPER VERSATILE. EVERYTHING, including the kombu, dried anchovies, and powdered soy sauce, can be found at most Asian grocery stores or on Amazon. After that it's just a matter of grinding everything together. I make a batch and place some in a salt-shaker for easy deployment. Sprinkle some in a soup that tastes too bland, or incorporate it in a dry rub for your next steak.

Note: Powdered soy is soy sauce that's been dehydrated, making it especially useful for dry spice blends like this one. And because granulated garlic sometimes contains MSG or salt, I prefer to use minced garlic that's been dried; it's also sometimes labeled as garlic flakes. If you can't find it at your local grocer, it is available on Amazon.

- **4 ounces kombu**
- **8 ounces dried shiitake mushrooms**
- **2 ounces dried anchovies**
- ¼ cup dried minced garlic or garlic flakes
- **2½ tablespoons powdered soy sauce** (see Sources, page 248, and headnote) or sea salt
- 1½ tablespoons freshly ground white pepper

1. Preheat the oven to 350°F.
2. Lay the kombu in a single layer on a baking sheet and place in the oven for 10 minutes. It will crisp and darken slightly. Remove it from the oven and let cool for a few minutes.
3. Crumble the kombu and place it, along with the rest of the ingredients, in a spice grinder or a blender and blend.
4. This will store very well, covered, for up to 6 months.

# UMAMI MASTER SAUCE

**MAKES ABOUT 3 CUPS**

THIS GLUTAMATE-INTENSE SAUCE CAN BE USED for wet applications, like braises and stews and any other dish that cooks low and slow. Since it's a concentrated sauce with several umami ingredients, a little bit goes a long way. Use a small amount and dilute as necessary.

- 2 cups top-quality tamari or soy sauce
- ¼ cup plus 2 tablespoons sherry wine
- ¼ cup dried wild mushrooms, like porcini
- ¼ cup red or white miso
- ¼ cup honey
- 1 tablespoon Marmite
- 1 tablespoon shio koji
- Hot sauce
- 1 (4-by-4-inch) piece dried kombu

1. Start with the tamari or soy sauce, in a pan over medium heat; do not let boil. Add the sherry wine, dried wild mushrooms, and miso. Stir.

2. Add the honey, Marmite, shio koji, some hot sauce, and the dried kombu. Stir for a minute, remove from the heat, and strain. Add water to taste to dilute its intensity, then cool.

3. Store, covered, in glass jars for up to around 6 months in your pantry.

# UMAMI KETCHUP

**MAKES 4 CUPS**

**I**T MAY SEEM LIKE A LOT OF EFFORT TO MAKE YOUR OWN ketchup from scratch when you could just grab a bottle the next time you're at the market, but trust me: This is worth it. The Umami Ketchup is super savory and makes even the blandest french fries taste amazing.

- 1 (28-ounce) can whole tomatoes in puree
- ¼ cup plus 2 tablespoons olive oil
- 2 medium onions, chopped
- ¼ cup tomato paste
- 2 cups packed dark brown sugar
- 1 cup cider vinegar
- 1½ teaspoons sea salt
- Dash of Worcestershire sauce
- Dash of fish sauce
- Pinch of truffle salt (optional)
- Pinch of Umami Master Dust (page 32)
- 1 teaspoon Umami Master Sauce (page 34)

1. Puree the tomatoes, including the juice from the can, in a blender until smooth.

2. Place the oil in a heavy saucepan over medium heat and when it's smoking, add the onions and cook, stirring often, until softened, about 8 minutes. Add the pureed tomatoes, tomato paste, brown sugar, vinegar, and sea salt and simmer, uncovered, over low heat, stirring occasionally, until the whole thing is very thick, about 1 hour. Toward the end of the cooking time, stir more frequently to prevent the ketchup from scorching.

3. Back to the blender. Puree the ketchup in batches until smooth. Chill, covered, overnight to allow the flavors to develop. Add the Worcestershire, fish sauce, truffle salt, if using, Umami Master Dust, and Umami Master Sauce.

4. Stored, covered, in the fridge, the ketchup will keep for up to 2 months.

# BASICS

## AND

# CONDIMENTS

# BLISTERED TOMATOES

**MAKES ABOUT ½ CUP**

**T**OMATOES NATURALLY HAVE A LOT OF GLUTAMATES, and if you blister them to trigger the Maillard reaction, you'll bring out even more of their natural umami. Using oil from the Garlic Confit is not mandatory, but if you have it, it adds a nice garlicky flavor to the tomatoes. I use cherry tomatoes in this recipe, but the method works using whole tomatoes, too.

- **1 pint cherry tomatoes**
- **Sea salt and freshly ground black pepper**
- **Oil from Garlic Confit** (page 38) **or extra-virgin olive oil**

1. Preheat the oven to 325°F.

2. Halve the tomatoes and place them in a large ovenproof skillet, preferably cast-iron. Season with salt and pepper to taste, then spoon in enough oil to coat the tomatoes generously. Arrange them in the skillet, cut side down, and roast for 30 to 45 minutes, until their skins shrivel and char slightly and the tomatoes collapse slightly upon themselves.

3. Store the blistered tomatoes in a covered container in the fridge for up to a day.

# CARAMELIZED ONIONS

**MAKES AS MANY ONIONS AS YOU'D LIKE**

**T**HINK OF CARAMELIZED ONIONS ON YOUR BURGER. That's a blast of umami right there. In addition to burgers, I put Caramelized Onions on my pizza, in my sandwiches, in my tacos . . . the possibilities are endless. It's very easy to make caramelized onions; in fact the technique you're exercising most here is patience, because they will take some time on the stove. But it is well worth the time to do it, and to do it right. You will be amply rewarded.

- As many yellow onions as you want to caramelize
- 1 tablespoon olive oil per onion

1. Begin by peeling and halving the onions, then thinly slice them. Heat the olive oil in a large saucepan over medium-low heat and, when it's rippling, add the onions. Stir them a bit, then let the onions do their thing. Every once in a while, give them a good stir. The onions will slowly break down and take on a beautiful dark-brown shade as they caramelize. Don't rush this process; if you do, you'll burn the onions instead of caramelizing them. If you find that the onions are browning too quickly, turn the heat down to low.

2. In total this will take 45 minutes or more; the darker, the sweeter, the better.

3. The onions store well, so I usually make one big batch and fridge the leftovers for use throughout the week.

# VADOUVAN

**MAKES 1 CUP**

- ½ teaspoon crushed Calabrian chilies (see headnote); or any small fresh red chile
- 8 garlic cloves, peeled
- 2 large onions (about 1 pound), chopped
- ½ pound shallots, peeled and halved
- 1 tablespoon olive oil
- 2 teaspoons ground cumin
- 1 teaspoon mustard seeds
- ½ teaspoon ground fenugreek (or whole fenugreek that you grind fresh in your spice mill; see Note)
- ½ teaspoon ground turmeric
- ¼ teaspoon freshly ground nutmeg
- ⅛ teaspoon ground cloves
- 1½ teaspoons sea salt
- ½ teaspoon freshly ground black pepper

**I** F YOU LIKE SMOKY, SAVORY SPICES, YOU WILL love vadouvan. Vadouvan is a blend of French and Indian flavors, with the classic French ingredients of onions, shallots, and garlic combining with spices that form the base of many Indian curry powders. My version adds a bit of an Italian element with Calabrian chilies, which have a distinct smokiness and heat. These chilies are usually sold in jars at Italian markets, at specialty shops like Williams-Sonoma, and, of course, on Amazon (see Sources, page 248).

Add vadouvan to dry rubs and marinades. It's even great sprinkled on fried eggs.

1. Preheat the oven to 350°F.

2. Place the Calabrian chilies in a food processor with the garlic and process until minced. Add the onions and shallots and pulse just a few times to chop coarsely.

3. Place a large skillet on medium-high. When the pan gets very hot or starts to smoke, add the olive oil, wait a minute, then add the mix from the processor. Reduce the heat to medium-low. Cook for 15 to 20 minutes, just until the onions start to brown. Don't step away from the stove: Keep stirring so things don't burn, scraping up anything that sticks to the bottom. Once the onions start to brown, toss in everything else—the cumin, mustard seeds, fenugreek, turmeric, nutmeg, cloves, salt, and pepper—and give it all a good stir to combine. Turn off the heat and set the pan aside.

4. Place a sheet of parchment paper or a Silpat mat on a baking sheet (if you're using parchment, spray or brush a light layer of olive oil on top). Spread the onion mixture onto the parchment or Silpat mat in a single layer so it will dehydrate evenly.

5. Drizzle or spray olive oil on top and bake until the onions have browned well and are pretty much dry all the way through, between 1 and 1½ hours, stirring often and rotating the pan about halfway through so everything bakes evenly. Break up any big clumps as you go along. Check it regularly and trust your senses: If something smells like it might be burning, it probably is!

6. Once the mixture is dried out well, set it aside to cool. Using a spoon or your fingers, break up any of the larger pieces, then funnel the spice into a jar or resealable bag and store.

7. The seasoning keeps well, so make a big batch. It keeps in the fridge for up to a month. It'll be fine in the freezer for up to 6 months.

**NOTE**

Fenugreek is a spice common to Indian, Middle Eastern, and North African cooking. You usually can find it at Indian markets; if not, check Whole Foods or another specialty grocer.

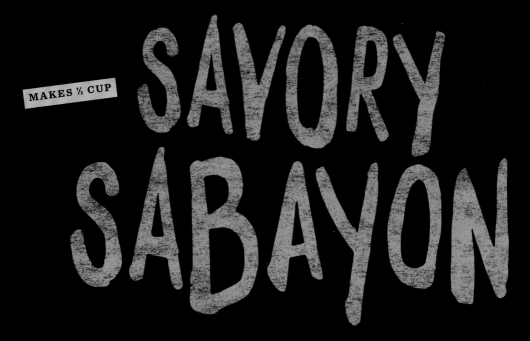

MAKES ½ CUP

# SAVORY SABAYON

**S**ABAYON IS TRADITIONALLY A FOAMY SAUCE THAT IS whipped up and served with berries for dessert. I took that idea and made it a savory sauce, balanced with a little sweetness thanks to the sweet wine (I like to use a sweet sherry like Pedro Ximénez P.X.; a Madeira or Marsala wine will also work). It's an all-purpose sauce that's great on roasted vegetables and potatoes and comes together in minutes.

- **2 large egg yolks**
- **2 tablespoons Umami Master Sauce** (page 34)
- **2 tablespoons sweet wine, like sweet sherry, such as Pedro Ximénez P.X.; Madeira;** or Marsala
- **2 tablespoons heavy cream or crème fraîche**

1. Whisk the yolks in the top of a double boiler set over simmering water. If you don't have a double boiler, you can easily make one by setting a heatproof bowl or pan over a saucepan filled with some simmering water.

2. When the eggs are foamy, which should take 5 to 7 minutes, add the Umami Master Sauce and wine. Whisk for 5 more minutes, or until the eggs are thick but still liquidy, then remove from the heat and add the cream. Stir to combine.

3. Serve warm.

# Seasoning: The Importance of Timing

**E**ARLY ON WHEN I FIRST started cooking, I made a stew that I forgot to season at the beginning. I figured no big deal—I could just salt it at the end. I was wrong. Even with the seasoning at the finish, the stew still tasted bland.

As it turns out, food needs the cooking process to absorb salt and other seasonings. But it's not just about seasoning early: It's also about seasoning throughout. To really bring out the flavor of any dish, it's crucial to salt the dish in the beginning, sometimes in the middle, and very often at the end. A final seasoning like a great sea salt right before you serve the dish seals the deal.

Season lightly in the beginning. Then, in the middle of the process, taste again. Some of the seasonings may have been absorbed; some may have cooked off. And remember, salt levels increase as things reduce, so you may have to adjust the other seasonings in the dish to compensate. If at any time you've realized you've oversalted, you can always add cream, vegetable puree, or flour, which are all neutral ingredients that will bring everything back into balance.

Finally, when everything's done, taste one more time. You probably will need to adjust the seasonings again, or reseason to really make the flavors pop.

And if you're having the dish as leftovers, it'll probably taste different than when you originally made it, because the flavors change after a night's rest in the fridge. A quick adjustment will do the trick. Trust your instincts. Let your palate be your guide.

# BURNT MISO

**MAKES AS MUCH AS YOU'D LIKE**

**A** COUPLE OF RAMEN SHOPS IN LOS ANGELES HAVE BURNT MISO ramen on their menu, which is what got me thinking that burning the miso—literally—might work in other dishes and even in cocktails. As it turns out, it works really, really well. The sharp bitterness that comes from charring contrasts nicely with the miso's inherent sweetness. Think of it like adding bitters to a sweet cocktail: The bitters modulate the drink for the better. Burn any type of miso for this recipe.

• **Miso, as much as you want to burn**

1. Preheat the oven to 400°F.

2. Spread a ½-inch layer of miso on a Silpat mat or a sheet of parchment paper on a baking sheet. Bake it for 30 minutes, or until the miso has a nice char on it. Cut off the burnt edges and keep the center. It'll smell and taste intensely savory.

3. Bring the miso back to its paste state by pureeing it in a blender or food processor before combining with other ingredients.

4. To store, place the puree in an airtight container and keep in the fridge. It'll be good for up to a month.

# PARMESAN BREAD CRUMBS

## MAKES 2 CUPS

**T**HESE ARE A STEP UP FROM YOUR USUAL BREAD crumbs thanks to the umami flavor from Parmesan and a light crunch courtesy of panko, which you can find at most grocery stores. It's great for topping off your mac and cheese or any other pasta; also throw it in your salads, sprinkle it on top of eggs, or add it to any other dish where you want crunch with a punch.

- 1 cup panko bread crumbs
- **1 cup (4 ounces) freshly grated Parmigiano-Reggiano**
- 2 tablespoons oil from Garlic Confit (page 38) or olive oil

1. In a small bowl, combine the panko, cheese, and oil. It's ready to use as is, or you can also toast the crumbs by placing them in a small skillet over medium-low heat. Sauté until the crumbs are lightly toasted and the cheese crisps, just a few minutes. Set aside and cool briefly before using.

2. Use what you need, then store the leftovers in a jar or other airtight container. It'll be good for up to a week.

# Cook from Your Palate Memory!

**W**HEN YOU THINK ABOUT the best pizza or burger you've ever had, what do you taste? What do you remember about where you were and who you were with and what you saw when you tasted it? There, that's it. Your palate memory. It's the flavor database of your recollections, not just the taste of the pizza or burger but also the experience you had while eating it. It's the flavor distilled into an ideal, a memory to chase again. Using your palate is something you can improve by practicing, like a sport. It doesn't just rely on your past experiences but improves over time as you travel the world and sample its wares.

If you think more broadly about all the most delicious things you've eaten, I bet you'd recall some simple everyday meals as well as highbrow tasting menus. Memory is indiscriminate: It takes the best and leaves the rest. At the highest level and the lowest, it is flavor—and often an *umami* flavor—that unites your memories. Your first lobster roll; a piece of cheese from the pan, fried and hard; or the snap of a great hot dog.

Those memories are all you need to start cooking with umami flavors. Really, that's it. When I ask myself what I want to eat, I never think, "I feel like having a meat dish right now." Instead I recall a moment of eating bliss and try to re-create that, in some form or another. And everything I do in the kitchen, from what I buy to how I umamify a dish to the techniques I use, serves my desire to re-create that moment.

So when you cook at home, focus on those core flavors. Resist following a recipe exactly (even my recipes!) or complicating a dish if it doesn't serve your palate memory. In the end it's all about what the flavors are saying. It's just up to you to listen.

# APPS AND LITTLE MEALS

**S**TART OFF WITH A LITTLE—OR A LOT—
of umami. These appetizers will kick off your meal
with a ton of delicious flavor.

*Highlighted ingredients are staples of the Umami Pantry
(page 24).*

# RAREBIT

**SERVES 1
HUNGRY DRUNK,
OR 2 AS A SNACK**

**O**NCE YOU KNOW WHAT TO LOOK FOR, YOU START TO NOTICE umami ingredients everywhere, especially in classic dishes where you might not otherwise expect to find them. The British dish rarebit, a classic pub dish, is like pizza and burgers—an umami bomb. Essentially melted cheese sauce on toast, rarebit has umami in the form of Worcestershire and aged cheese.

I added the Umami Master Sauce to intensify the flavor a little without overpowering the sauce; that plus the Worcestershire will cut through and complement the bitterness of the beer. The beer, by the way, is the backbone of rarebit, so you want something that's strong and hearty, like a good-quality porter or a dark ale.

- 1 tablespoon unsalted butter, plus more for the bread
- 2 slices of your favorite whole-grain sandwich bread or loaf
- 1 tablespoon all-purpose flour
- ¼ cup whole milk
- ½ cup porter, amber, or other brown beer
- 1 teaspoon dry mustard
- ½ teaspoon Umami Master Sauce (page 34)
- ⅛ teaspoon freshly ground black pepper
- 6 ounces aged sharp cheddar, preferably English, grated
- Worcestershire sauce

1. Preheat the broiler.

2. Butter both sides of the bread slices and toast each side in a skillet over medium heat until lightly browned, about 2 minutes per side. You'll be broiling the toast, so if you have it, use a cast-iron skillet or a similar pan that can go from the stovetop directly to the broiler.

3. While the bread toasts, place the tablespoon of butter in a medium saucepan over low heat. As the butter melts, add the flour and whisk for a minute to create a very light roux. Pour in the milk and beer.

4. Give the liquids a quick stir, then add the dry mustard, Umami Master Sauce, black pepper, cheddar cheese, and a long dash of Worcestershire. Stir until the cheese melts, about 2 minutes.

5. Arrange the toasts side by side in the skillet. Pour or spoon the cheese sauce over the toasts and place the skillet under the broiler. Broil just until the cheese starts to bubble and brown a bit, a minute or two. Serve hot. This is perfect beer food, so pour yourself a pint to wash it all down with.

# CRAB IMPERIAL

I GREW UP IN MARYLAND, where I enjoyed crab everything, including crab imperial. This is a classic, but rarely seen anymore, dish that's sort of like a crab cake baked up as a casserole. In my version the umami-bearing crab and Parmesan Bread Crumbs are kicked up a notch by the classic umami sidekick sherry.

Since crab is the star of the show here, invest in fresh crabmeat if you can; otherwise source high-quality canned crabmeat.

**SERVES 4**

- 2 tablespoons unsalted butter
- 2 tablespoons all-purpose flour
- ¾ cup whole milk
- 1 large garlic clove, peeled and lightly crushed
- 2 large egg yolks
- ⅓ cup dry sherry
- 1 teaspoon Dijon mustard
- ½ teaspoon dry mustard
- ½ teaspoon sea salt
- ⅛ teaspoon Piment d'Espelette or cayenne pepper
- 2 pounds lump crabmeat
- 2 tablespoons finely chopped fresh flat-leaf parsley
- ½ cup Parmesan Bread Crumbs (page 48), untoasted

1. Preheat the oven to 450°F, with the rack in the upper third.

2. Make a béchamel: Melt the butter in a small, heavy saucepan over medium-low heat. Add the flour and whisk for about 2 minutes, until the flour is well incorporated. In a slow stream, whisk in the milk, then add the garlic. Raise the heat to medium and bring the mixture to a boil, still whisking, then reduce it back to low and simmer, whisking, until the béchamel is thickened, about 3 minutes. Remove from the heat and discard the garlic. Set aside.

3. In a medium bowl, whisk together the yolks, sherry, mustards, salt, and Piment d'Espelette, then add the hot béchamel in a slow stream, still whisking. Pour this mixture back into the saucepan and cook over very low heat, whisking constantly, until an instant-read thermometer registers 160°F, about 2 minutes. Remove the pan from the heat and gently stir in the crabmeat and parsley. Pour into a large cast-iron skillet (or, if you have a couple small cast-iron pans or large ramekins, you can divide the mixture into individual portions).

4. Sprinkle the Parmesan Bread Crumbs liberally over the crab to coat. Bake until the crab is bubbling and the crumbs are golden brown, about 5 minutes. Remove from the oven and set the skillet on the table so everyone can serve themselves, or heap a generous spoonful onto everyone's plate.

# SALMON
## in TOMATO-TRUFFLE BUTTER

SERVES 4

**T**HIS FRENCH DISH IS INSPIRED BY THE CHEF MARCO PIERRE WHITE and his French forbears. White opened a French restaurant called Harveys in the late 1980s in London, where he gained critical acclaim and became one of the first superstar chefs. One of his famous dishes is a fillet of salmon poached in a tomato sauce; I riff on that idea, poaching the salmon in duck fat, which adds umami and flavor without overcooking the fish due to the low heat and insulation the duck fat provides.

Note: You can find tubes of truffle puree at specialty markets or online at Amazon (see Sources, page 248). If you don't have any on hand, use Umami Master Sauce instead.

- **1 pint duck fat or goose fat**
- 8 ounces wild salmon fillet, trimmed of all skin and fat
- **1 pint cherry tomatoes**
- 3 tablespoons unsalted butter
- Sea salt and freshly ground black pepper
- **1 tablespoon truffle puree** (see headnote) **or Umami Master Sauce** (page 34)
- 1 teaspoon fresh orange juice, plus more if needed
- 1 teaspoon best-quality olive oil

. . . . . . . . . . . . . . . . . . . . . . . . . . . .

OPTIONAL GARNISHES
- Fresh chives, chopped
- 1 avocado, sliced

1. Place the fat in a medium saucepan over low heat until simmering.

2. Meanwhile, take the salmon and carefully slice it crosswise into 4 equal pieces. Set aside while you prepare the sauce.

3. Place the tomatoes in a blender and blend until they're completely smooth.

4. Strain the tomatoes into a small saucepan and put the heat on low. Add the butter and stir until it's well incorporated.

5. Season with salt and pepper to taste. Stir in the truffle puree or Umami Master Sauce. Add a few drops of orange juice and the olive oil. Taste and add more orange juice if necessary. Whisk well until it's a shiny pink sauce.

6. Put the salmon in the simmering fat for 2 to 3 minutes, just to warm and poach it very slightly.

7. Spoon some sauce onto a large dinner plate and add the salmon on top (don't discard the fat—stick it back in the fridge or freezer and save to use again with another fish dish). Place the remaining sauce in a bowl for serving. If you'd like, garnish with a few whole chives and avocado slices. Serve immediately with the sauce on the side so guests can help themselves to more if they'd like.

# ROASTED FINGERLING POTATOES
## STUFFED WITH SMOKED TROUT MOUSSE

SERVES 4

**S**MOKING FISH GIVES IT A DEPTH OF UMAMI FLAVOR, MAKING IT an ideal complement to something that doesn't pack as much of a punch, like potatoes. Here I take some smoked trout—you can also use hot-smoked salmon if you want—and mix it with cream cheese to make a mousse that's then piped (or spooned) into potato shells. The result is an elegant appetizer that seems more complicated than it really is. If you're feeling luxurious, add a little caviar on top before serving.

---

- **1 pound fingerling potatoes**
- **Olive oil**
- **Sea salt**
- **½ teaspoon fresh thyme leaves** (from about 2 sprigs)
- **1 smoked trout with the skin removed, crumbled** (about 8 ounces)
- **6 ounces cream cheese, at room temperature**
- **1 teaspoon prepared horseradish**
- **1 tablespoon half-and-half or heavy cream, plus more for thinning**

. . . . . . . . . . . .

### GARNISHES

- **Fresh chervil, chopped**
- **Piment d'Espelette or cayenne pepper** (optional)
- **Caviar** (if you really want to gild the lily)

1. Preheat the oven to 350°F.

2. Place the fingerling potatoes in a baking dish or on a baking sheet and coat with olive oil. Season generously with salt and thyme. Bake until the potatoes are fork tender—start checking them at around 30 minutes—then take them out of the oven and cool.

3. While the potatoes roast, pulse the smoked trout, cream cheese, horseradish, and half-and-half or cream in a food processor. You want the mixture to have the texture of whipped cream, so add more half-and-half or cream bit by bit to thin it out as much as you need to. Be careful not to overprocess or it won't have the right texture. Place the mousse mixture into a pastry bag fitted with a star tip, if you have one; otherwise, set the mix aside.

4. When the potatoes are cool, cut them lengthwise and scoop out some of the centers. Pipe or spoon the mousse into the potatoes. Garnish with the chervil and, if you have it, the piment d'espelette or cayenne pepper. If you are feeling luxurious, add the caviar, too. Serve.

# BALTIMORE CODDIES

**SERVES 4 AS AN APPETIZER OR LIGHT DINNER**

- ½ pound salt cod
- 1 pound Yukon gold potatoes, peeled and chopped into equal-sized pieces
- 2 tablespoons whole milk
- ¼ cup crushed saltine crackers (6 to 10 crackers)
- ½ teaspoon freshly ground black pepper
- 2 large eggs
- Dash of fish sauce
- Dash of Worcestershire sauce
- Vegetable oil, for frying

. . . . . . . . . . . . . . . .

**FOR SERVING**

- 8 saltine crackers or 4 slider buns
- Yellow mustard

ONE OF BALTIMORE'S MOST TREAsured culinary creations is the coddie. It's basically a croquette of fish—the "coddie" is salt cod—and potatoes sandwiched between two saltine crackers. It's usually eaten as a snack after school, and this is a classic rendition. It's delicious as an appetizer or light dinner.

Start 1 day ahead to allow for soaking the cod.

1. The day before making the coddies, soak the fish in a bowl of water in the fridge for 24 hours, changing the water every 6 to 8 hours.

2. The next day, place the fish in a large skillet and pour in just enough water to cover it completely. Simmer over low heat for 10 to 15 minutes or until it's soft and flaky, then drain. Using a fork, shred the fish and set it aside to cool.

3. Place the potatoes in a large pot and cover with water. Bring to a boil and boil until the potatoes are cooked through and yield easily when pierced with a fork, 15 to 20 minutes.

4. When the potatoes are done, drain, place them in a large bowl with the milk, and mash.

5. Add the salt cod to the mashed potatoes, along with the crushed crackers, the pepper, eggs, and dashes of fish sauce and Worcestershire, and stir well to combine. Scoop out a big spoonful of the mix, place it on a work surface, and, using the palm of your hand, press down slightly to flatten it so it will fit on the cracker or the bun. You could go thinner and slightly larger than the cracker or bun if you want, just bear in mind that you don't want to flatten the coddies *too* much. If they're too thin, they'll fall apart as you fry them.

6. Place a cooling rack on a baking sheet next to the stove or your frying area to drain the coddies after frying.

7. In a large cast-iron skillet or other pan that you can use for pan-frying, pour in ¼ inch of vegetable oil and turn the heat to medium. When the oil is hot enough—you'll know it's ready when a little piece of the coddie mix sizzles when you drop it in—carefully add the coddies, working with just a few at a time as necessary to avoid crowding the pan. Cook each side of the coddies until golden brown and crisp, 4 to 6 minutes per side, then remove the coddies to the rack to drain. Cook the remaining coddies, heating more oil between batches as needed.

8. Here comes the fun part: assembly. Everyone can do their own if they want. Place a coddie on a saltine cracker or bottom slider bun, squeeze some mustard on top, and finish it off with another saltine or the top bun. That's it. The coddies are great while they're still warm, but they're also good at room temp.

# DUCK RILLETTES

**SERVES 2 TO 4**

**R**ILLETTES OFTEN SHOW UP ON THE CHARCUTERIE BOARDS OF the fanciest restaurants in town, but you'll be surprised at how ridiculously easy they are to make yourself. For the uninitiated, rillettes are a creamy pâté made with shredded meat that's been poached in its own fat. Usually that shredded meat is pork, but here I use duck, which has wonderful flavor. You can get duck confit in gourmet shops or online (see Sources, page 248). The duck fat also adds a luxurious richness to what is generally a traditionally rustic spread.

- **2 cups shredded meat from duck confit** (see headnote)

- **2 tablespoons minced shallots**

- **1 tablespoon chopped fresh flat-leaf parsley, plus extra for garnish**

- **1 tablespoon chopped fresh thyme**

- **2 tablespoons brandy**

- **Sea salt and freshly ground black pepper**

- **Up to 1 cup duck fat, melted and slightly cooled**

- **1 tablespoon unsalted butter** (optional)

- **Toast points, for serving**

1. In a large bowl with an electric mixer, combine the duck meat, shallots, the 1 tablespoon parsley, the thyme, and brandy, and cream together for 2 minutes. Season with a pinch of salt and freshly ground pepper.

2. Mixing all the while, pour in the duck fat in a slow, steady stream, until everything is well combined and moist; it shouldn't take more than a cup to get the right consistency. Taste, and adjust seasonings if necessary. For extra richness, mix in the tablespoon of butter.

3. Serve with toast points, garnished with parsley.

4. Refrigerated in an airtight container, this will keep for 3 days.

# FETTUNTA

**F**ETTUNTA IS GRILLED GARLICKED AND OILED BREAD, the Italian version of the French *tartine*.

The type of bread you'll want for your fettunta depends on the toppings. The toppings I have here, a *bagna cauda* and a raclette, are hearty, so I like to use bread that's equally sturdy, like a rustic boule. Of course you can use sourdough in a pinch.

In addition to preparing these to order, you can make the fettunta for a party. Instead of assembling each slice of bread individually, prepare a big batch of each topping and set them out on the table, along with the grilled bread. Your guests can pick and choose and build their own fettunta.

# BAGNA CAUDA FETTUNTA

SERVES 4

**B**AGNA CAUDA IS USUALLY translated as "hot bath," and it's a classic dish from the Piedmont region of Italy where anchovies and garlic are bathed in warm olive oil until the flavors meld into a beautiful dip. My version turns it into a topping; with the anchovies and blistered cherry tomatoes, this is a very umami-intense fettunta.

- 7 garlic cloves, peeled
- ¼ cup extra-virgin olive oil, plus more for brushing the bread
- 8 tablespoons (1 stick) unsalted butter
- ¼ cup anchovy fillets, rinsed
- Freshly ground black pepper
- 4 slices boule or other hearty loaf
- ½ cup whole-milk ricotta
- 1½ cups Blistered Tomatoes (page 40)

1. Preheat a grill to high heat.

2. To make the sauce, slice 6 of the garlic cloves paper-thin.

3. Heat the oil and butter in a small saucepan over low heat until they've warmed and the butter foams. Add the garlic, anchovy fillets, and a crack of pepper and cook for 5 minutes. Transfer to a food processor or blender and puree.

4. Now, assemble the fettunta. Cut the remaining garlic clove in half. Brush each side of the bread slices with olive oil. Toast the bread on the cool part of your grill or in a skillet set on your stove over medium heat, then rub the halved garlic clove on each side. Place the bread on a cutting board.

5. Spread as much of the bagna cauda on each slice of bread as you'd like, then top each with 2 tablespoons of the ricotta. Pile the blistered tomatoes on top. Serve.

6. If you have leftovers, the remaining bagna cauda can be refrigerated for up to 3 days. It also can be used as a dip for raw vegetables.

# RACLETTE FETTUNTA

SERVES 4

**R**ACLETTE IS A SEMI-HARD CHEESE THAT MELTS WELL AND IS GREAT for fettunta. Note that this cheese is particularly salty, so you won't need to add any more salt to the toast. To balance the strength of the cheese, I also top the bread with fingerling potatoes, which have a creamy texture and flavor that pair well with cheese. You can also use any young potato instead; just avoid starchy taters like Russets.

- 4 fingerling potatoes, cut into ⅛-inch slices
- Extra-virgin olive oil
- Sea salt and freshly ground black pepper
- ½ pound raclette cheese
- 4 slices boule or other hearty loaf
- 1 garlic clove, halved
- 8 slices prosciutto
- ½ cup Caramelized Onions (page 41)

1. Preheat the oven to 350°F.

2. Place the potatoes in a baking dish or on a baking sheet. Drizzle enough oil over the potatoes to coat them generously. Season them with salt and pepper and roast until soft, about 20 minutes. Set aside.

3. When the potatoes finish roasting, melt the cheese in a small nonstick pan over low heat and set aside. Alternatively, you can melt the cheese in a pan set on the cool part of your grill while you grill the bread.

4. Preheat a grill to high heat.

5. To grill the bread, brush each side of each slice with olive oil and place on the grill. When the slices are nice and toasted, remove from the grill and rub the halved garlic clove on both sides of each slice. Top with the potatoes, prosciutto, Caramelized Onions, melted cheese, and a turn or two from the pepper mill. Serve.

# UMAMI-LAYERED TART

**MAKES FOUR 3-INCH TARTS**

**W**ITH BEEF TARTARE, mushroom duxelles, and roasted tomatoes stacked atop a Parmesan crust, these tarts are an elegant, reconceived version of my original Umami Burger (page 104).

There are multiple components that will take a little bit of organization and time, but none of them are difficult to execute, and if you want to break up the work, you can make the Parmesan crisps, the mushroom layer, and the beef tartare ahead. That said, because of the time involved, save these tarts for a special dinner party occasion. Your efforts will be rewarded handsomely with the tarts' wow factor.

### THE BEEF LAYER

The beef is a tartare that needs to be marinated for a few hours or overnight, but if you prefer something quicker, you can use leftovers from the Sweet and Savory Brisket (page 174). For a pescatarian version, use cubed sashimi-grade tuna instead.

- ¼ cup Umami Master Sauce (page 34)
- ½ teaspoon Umami Master Dust (page 32)
- 1 teaspoon sesame oil
- 1 teaspoon olive oil
- ¼ teaspoon fish sauce
- ¼ teaspoon balsamic vinegar
- Sea salt and freshly ground black pepper
- 12 ounces tenderloin, rib-eye, or New York strip steak, trimmed and cut into ¼-inch cubes

### THE ROASTED TOMATO LAYER

Be sure to use red tomatoes. The color is great for the tart.

- 4 red beefsteak tomatoes
- Sea salt and freshly ground black pepper
- 1 sprig thyme
- Extra-virgin olive oil

*continued*

### THE PARMESAN CRISPS (OPTIONAL)

Since there already is Parmesan in the tart dough, the Parmesan crisps are entirely optional. They give the tarts another texture.

- 3 ounces Parmigiano-Reggiano

### THE TART DOUGH

- 8 tablespoons (1 stick) cold unsalted butter
- 1¼ cups all-purpose flour, plus more for rolling out
- 8 ounces Parmigiano-Reggiano, grated (about 2 cups)
- 2 large egg yolks
- Sea salt

### THE MUSHROOM DUXELLES LAYER

I use a combination of white cremini mushrooms, shiitake mushrooms, and dried morels and porcinis, but feel free to customize and make your own mushroom mix.

- 1 cup water
- 1 ounce dried mushrooms
- 1 sprig thyme
- 15 ounces fresh mushrooms
- 2 tablespoons unsalted butter
- 1 teaspoon extra-virgin olive oil
- 1 shallot, chopped
- Drop of sesame oil
- Drop of soy sauce

### TO FINISH

- Sea salt and freshly ground black pepper
- Aged balsamic vinegar
- Chopped fresh sage, chervil, tarragon, or chives

1. **MAKE THE BEEF:** Stir together the Umami Master Sauce, Umami Master Dust, sesame oil, olive oil, fish sauce, balsamic vinegar, and a pinch of salt and pepper in a medium bowl. Mix in the beef and let marinate in the fridge for a few hours or overnight.

2. **MAKE THE TOMATOES:** On the day you plan to serve the tarts, preheat the oven to 325°F, with a rack in the middle.

3. Quarter the tomatoes and place them in a cast-iron skillet or casserole pan. Season with salt, pepper, and the thyme, then add enough glugs of olive oil to coat the tomatoes generously so they won't burn in the oven.

4. Roast the tomatoes until they shrink and their skins are easy to pull off, about 1 hour. Remove the tomatoes from the oven and discard the skins and thyme sprig (keep the oven on). Set the tomatoes aside. It you want, take a spoonful of the tomato liquid from the pan and add it to the beef that's marinating in the fridge. Reserve a few more spoonfuls to add to the mushroom duxelles.

5. If making the Parmesan crisps, increase the oven temperature to 375°F. Otherwise, increase the temperature to 350°F.

6. **MAKE THE OPTIONAL PARMESAN CRISPS:** Grate the Parmesan on the small-hole side of a four-sided box grater into a small bowl. Using a tablespoon measure, place the cheese in mounds at least 4 inches apart on a baking sheet lined with a Silpat mat or parchment paper. Flatten the mounds with the back of a spoon. Bake the cheese on the middle rack of the oven until the cheese is crisp and golden in color, 8 to 11 minutes, then remove the pan from the oven and let the crisps cool for 10 minutes. With a spatula, carefully transfer the crisps to a cooling rack to cool completely. The crisps can be made up to 2 days ahead and stored in an airtight container. This recipe makes more than you need; save the rest for an Umami Burger (page 104) or for snacking.

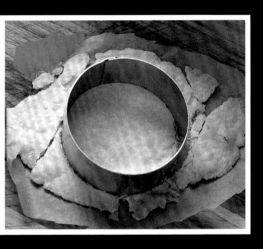

7. **MAKE THE TART DOUGH:** Start by cutting the butter into small pieces. Place the flour in a large bowl, then the butter, Parmesan cheese, egg yolks, and a pinch of salt. Using your hands, a dough cutter, or a mixer, combine until the dough comes together. Form the dough into a ball, wrap it tightly with plastic wrap, and place it in the fridge for 30 minutes.

8. **MEANWHILE, MAKE THE MUSHROOM DUXELLES:** Warm the water in a small pot over low heat. Turn off the heat, add the dried mushrooms and thyme, and let soak until the mushrooms have rehydrated, 20 to 30 minutes. Discard the thyme sprig and strain the liquid to remove any grit. Set the mushrooms and their liquid aside.

9. Slice the fresh mushrooms. If you're using shiitakes, stem them first (their stems are tough). Discard the stems.

10. Heat the butter and olive oil in a large skillet over medium heat. Add the shallot and cook for a few minutes until softened, then add the fresh mushrooms and cook, stirring, until the mushrooms are well seared. Add the rehydrated dried mushrooms along with their liquid and the reserved tomato liquid if you have it. Season with a drop of sesame oil and a dash of soy sauce. Stir. (See Flavor Tip, page 78.)

11. Reduce until all the liquid has evaporated, about 4 minutes. Place the mushrooms in a food processor and process just until they're coarsely chopped. Mushroom duxelles is always served at room temperature, so allow it to cool down before you begin layering the tarts. Set aside. The mushrooms can be made ahead and refrigerated, covered, for up to 2 days.

12. **BAKE THE TART BASE AND FINISH THE MUSHROOMS:** Flour a large piece of parchment. Pull the dough out from the fridge and place it on the floured parchment. Flour the top of the dough, then place another piece of parchment on top.

13. Using a rolling pin—a wine bottle will work just fine—roll out the dough about $\frac{1}{16}$ inch thick into a square roughly 6 inches by 6 inches.

14. Place the dough with the parchment back in the fridge.

15. Preheat the oven to 400°F.

16. Remove the dough from the fridge, discard the parchment on top, and place the dough, still on the bottom sheet of parchment, on a baking sheet. Set it in the oven and bake until it's golden in color, 8 to 10 minutes.

17. **LAYER, LAYER, LAYER:** Remove the tart base from the oven. With four 3-inch ring molds (or round cookie cutters, or even tuna cans with the tops and bottoms removed), cut out 4 neat circles and place each round on its own large serving plate.

18. Use the ring molds to provide structure as you build these layers. The first layer will be the mushroom duxelles: Spoon the mushrooms on top of the tart base, packing them tightly. Season with salt and pepper.

19. Next, add the beef, then the tomatoes. Press down on the tomatoes with the bottom of a can or back of a spoon to compact the layers.

20. Place the completed tarts in the fridge for 5 minutes to firm up (you can keep them in the fridge for up to 10 minutes; if they stay in there much longer, the tart bottoms may get soggy).

21. To serve, carefully remove the molds. Top each with a Parmesan crisp, if using. Drizzle on the aged balsamic and sprinkle with the herbs.

**FLAVOR TIP**

Pour in the liquids *after* the mushrooms have seared. As we know, a lot of flavor comes from the Maillard reaction and the browning process, so if we add the liquids too early, the mushrooms won't get a chance to sear and won't benefit from that extra depth of flavor.

# UMAMI STROMBOLI

**MAKES 1 ROLL; SERVES 6 TO 8**

**T**HIS STROMBOLI IS PERKED UP WITH SOME umami-intense ingredients like tomato paste and mushrooms. It also has black garlic, which is garlic that's been fermented for a period of time—usually around a month—to give it a complex, rich flavor. You can find it at specialty grocers, spice shops, Whole Foods, and Trader Joe's, or you can order it on Amazon.

Roll the stromboli up like a burrito, let it cool to room temp, then slice and pass around with stiff drinks at your next party.

## DOUGH

- 1½ teaspoons instant yeast
- 1 cup water
- Olive oil
- 2¼ cups bread flour or all-purpose flour
- ½ tablespoon sea salt

## FILLINGS

- 1 cup black olives, pitted
- 3 garlic cloves, preferably black garlic, peeled
- Olive oil
- ½ cup mushroom duxelles (page 74) or fresh shiitake mushrooms, stemmed and sliced
- Sea salt and freshly ground black pepper
- ½ cup tomato paste, or ½ cup Umami-Minded Tomato Sauce (page 128) that's been simmered over low heat for 20 minutes to remove most of its liquid
- 1 pound Italian sausages removed from casings or ground beef, crumbled and browned
- 4 Peppadew peppers (see page 248)
- Fresh thyme leaves from 3 sprigs thyme
- Freshly grated Parmigiano-Reggiano, fontina, or low-moisture mozzarella

## TOPPINGS

- 1 cup cherry tomatoes, halved
- Fresh thyme leaves
- Rosemary sprigs
- Parmigiano-Reggiano

*continued*

1. **MAKE THE DOUGH:** In the bowl of a stand mixer, combine the yeast, water, and 1½ tablespoons of olive oil. Add the bread flour or all-purpose flour all at once and, using the dough hook, mix on the mixer's lowest setting. After 5 minutes, step up the speed one notch to the second-to-lowest setting, and let it go for 5 more minutes, or until the dough comes together. Add a drizzle of olive oil and the salt, then mix for 1 minute or so to incorporate. (If you don't have a stand mixer, you can also knead this by hand.)

2. Cover the bowl and set the dough aside to rise until it doubles in size, about an hour. The exact time will depend on how cold or warm your kitchen is (the colder, the longer it takes). The dough will become elastic, sticky, and soft.

3. **MEANWHILE, MAKE THE FILLINGS:** Place the olives in a blender along with the garlic cloves and enough olive oil to liquefy, about ¼ cup. Puree until smooth. Set aside.

4. If you're using shiitake mushrooms instead of the duxelles, sauté them in 1 tablespoon of olive oil until they're soft, seasoning with salt and pepper.

5. **READY TO ROLL:** When the dough is close to doubling in size, preheat the oven to 375°F.

6. When the dough is ready, coat your hands with olive oil and pull the dough out of the bowl and onto your work surface. Prod and pull and stretch it with your fingers to form it into a rectangle roughly 10 inches by 16 inches and a quarter inch thick, with the longer side of the rectangle closest to you.

7. Keep a border of an inch or so on each side to make it easier to roll up later. Spoon the olive puree onto the left third of the rectangle, then, in the center third, the tomato paste or sauce, the meat, the Peppadews, and finally the mushrooms, leaving the right third bare. Sprinkle the thyme and a layer of cheese on top of the fillings, then season it all with a bit of salt and pepper.

8. Fold in the sides of the dough lengthwise; the sides should only partially cover the fillings. Carefully start rolling up the dough on the olive end and keep going until you have a nice, fat log. Crimp the ends to seal everything in.

9. Stud the top of the roll with the halved cherry tomatoes, then sprinkle the thyme leaves, rosemary sprigs, and a fresh grating of cheese on top. Line a baking sheet with parchment paper, then transfer the rolled dough to it.

10. Bake until the dough is completely cooked through, rotating the pan halfway through, about 45 minutes.

11. Let the stromboli cool to room temperature, discard the rosemary sprigs, then cut into slices. Serve.

# SOUPS
## AND
# SALADS

**S**ELECT UMAMI-FILLED INGREDIENTS AND combine them with some solid cooking techniques, and even the simplest soups and salads will burst with flavor. The recipes in this chapter will show you a few ways to do just that.

*Highlighted ingredients are staples of the Umami Pantry (page 24).*

# BLENDER GAZPACHO

**SERVES 4**

- 2 pounds very ripe tomatoes
- Olive oil
- 3 slices pain de mie, country loaf, or other bread, crusts removed
- Sherry vinegar
- ½ medium onion, peeled
- ½ medium cucumber, peeled
- 2 garlic cloves, peeled
- 1 green bell pepper, cored and seeded
- Sea salt and freshly ground black pepper
- Pinch of sugar
- Pimentón (smoked paprika) or red pepper flakes, for garnish

THE TOMATOES ARE BLENDED WITH THE other vegetables to make a smooth, creamy, pink gazpacho. Tomatoes have the most umami flavor when they're ripe, and are at their peak umami right off the vine. If you can find tomatoes on the vine at your farmers' market or grocer, grab a bunch and put them to good use here. I roast the tomatoes for a more complex flavor; it's an extra step, but worth it. The sherry vinegar is an umami sidekick that will amplify the umami.

1. Preheat the oven to 375°F.

2. Place the tomatoes on a baking sheet lined with parchment paper. Drizzle with enough olive oil to coat the tomatoes on all sides, then roast until their skins start to blister and they start to collapse a little bit, about 30 minutes. Don't overcook and dry out the tomatoes; you want some of their liquid in the gazpacho, too. Peel the skins off the tomatoes and discard. Remove the seeds, then chop the tomatoes coarsely. Place the tomatoes in a blender and set aside while you prep everything else.

3. Place the bread slices in a bowl or casserole dish and pour in just enough sherry vinegar to soak the bread. Meanwhile, dice the onion, cucumber, garlic cloves, and bell pepper. If you prefer a chunkier soup, reserve half of the diced veggies, refrigerate, and mix in at the very end before serving. Otherwise put all of the veggies in the blender with the tomatoes. Season with salt and pepper, then add 2 tablespoons of olive oil, 2 teaspoons of sherry vinegar, the sugar, and a big splash of water to thin it out.

4. Blend everything for a few seconds, then blend in the bread, in batches if everything doesn't fit in one go. Add more water if the gazpacho is too thick for your liking, or another tablespoon of olive oil if the soup isn't emulsifying and coming together.

5. Cover and chill the gazpacho in the fridge overnight. The next day, taste and readjust the seasonings. If you reserved half of the diced veggies, add them in now. Spoon into bowls and garnish with a pinch of the pimentón or red pepper flakes.

# MUSHROOM VELOUTÉ SOUP

**SERVES 6**

**A** VELOUTÉ IS MADE WITH STOCK, CREAM, AND WHITE WINE. This is my spin on the classic: I use dry sherry instead of white wine and add dried wild mushrooms to up the umami quotient for a super-flavorful stock. Button mushrooms don't have as much flavor as the dried mushrooms, but they have a lot more mass and a great meatiness that rounds out the soup.

The key to making this, or any other soup, is adding the liquid in stages. Add the sherry, then reduce; add the stock, then reduce; add the cream, then reduce. The result is a beautiful, rich soup. A small cup will be all you need to start your meal.

The soup has best flavor if made the day before you plan to serve it.

- 1 tablespoon Umami Master Sauce (page 34)
- 1 cup water
- ¼ cup dried porcini mushrooms, rinsed
- ¼ cup dried morel mushrooms, rinsed
- 2 tablespoons unsalted butter
- 1 shallot, chopped
- Sea salt
- 2½ cups (7 ounces) sliced button mushrooms
- 2 sprigs thyme
- 1 garlic clove, crushed

- 1 teaspoon extra-virgin olive oil
- Pinch of Umami Master Dust (page 32)
- Dash of soy sauce
- ½ cup dry sherry
- Freshly ground black pepper
- ½ cup heavy cream

**GARNISHES**

- Aged sherry or balsamic vinegar
- Chanterelles or other wild mushrooms, chopped and sautéed in butter (optional, if you want to gild the lily)

1.  Warm the master sauce and the water in a small saucepan over low heat, then turn the heat off and add the porcinis and morels. Soak the mushrooms until softened, 20 to 30 minutes. This will become the mushroom stock.

2.  Meanwhile, melt the butter in a large saucepan over medium heat. Add the shallot and a pinch of salt and cook for 2 minutes. The shallot should soften but not color, so take the pan off the heat if it seems like it is cooking too fast.

3.  Add the button mushrooms, thyme sprigs, garlic, and olive oil to the pan. Stir, then add the master dust and soy sauce. Cook, stirring, until the button mushrooms are nicely browned and soft enough to pierce with a fork, 5 to 7 minutes.

4.  Pour in the sherry and reduce it until it's almost all gone. Taste and season the mushrooms with salt and pepper.

5.  Strain the mushroom stock through a fine-mesh sieve or a coffee filter to remove any grit from the mushrooms, then add the liquids and the rehydrated mushrooms to the pan with the button mushrooms. Bring it all to a boil. When it's reduced by about half, about 4 minutes, add the cream.

6.  When the cream has reduced by half, about 5 minutes, discard the thyme sprigs and carefully transfer everything to a blender or a food processor. You don't want to completely fill the blender or processor with the hot liquid, so work in batches if necessary.

7.  Start by blending on low, then rev it up. Blend for a few minutes, until it's smooth and completely emulsified. Taste. Season with salt and pepper if needed.

8.  I like the velouté to be thick yet still loose. If your soup has a thicker consistency than you'd like, add a little water to thin it out, then reblend. If the soup is too thin, put it back on the stove and reduce until it hits your preferred consistency.

9.  To serve, divide the soup among small bowls or demitasse cups. Garnish with a drizzle of the aged vinegar and the sautéed wild mushrooms, if using.

# NONTRADITIONAL UMAMI-SPIKED CHOWDER

**SERVES 4**

EVERYONE HAS A FAVORITE CLAM CHOWDER. HERE'S MINE, made with most of the traditional New England clam chowder ingredients (onion, clam juice, and milk) and spiked with a good grating of Parmesan from the Umami Pantry, along with some truffle if you really want to go all out. This comforting chowder gets its velvety thickness from pureed potato, not heavy cream, which lets the flavors shine through more. As for the clams themselves, littleneck clams are traditional, but use whatever is local.

- 1 large onion, chopped
- 2 tablespoons unsalted butter
- 2 large Yukon gold potatoes (about 12 ounces), peeled and chopped
- Sea salt and freshly ground black pepper
- ¼ cup plus 2 tablespoons dry white wine or sake
- 16 ounces bottled clam juice
- 1 cup whole milk
- 2 tablespoons freshly grated Parmigiano-Reggiano
- 24 clams in shells (see headnote), scrubbed
- ½ black truffle or 1 teaspoon preserved black truffle (optional; see page 26), sliced thin or grated on a Microplane
- Chopped fresh flat-leaf parsley

1. Cook the onion in the butter in a Dutch oven or large saucepan over medium heat until soft, 5 to 7 minutes. Add the potatoes and season with a generous pinch of salt and pepper. Deglaze the pan with the wine or sake until it's fully reduced, about 3 minutes. Add the clam juice, milk, and Parmesan and simmer for 10 minutes, then kill the heat.

2. When it's cooled a bit, put it in a blender and blend it all together, in batches if you need to, until smooth. Return the chowder to the Dutch oven or saucepan and reheat over low heat. Add the clams and the truffle, if using, and cover and cook until the clams open. When the clams open, remove the meat from the shells, returning the meat to the chowder, and ladle the chowder into bowls. Garnish with parsley and serve.

# CREAMY SALAD DRESSING with MiXED GREENS

**SERVES 4;
MAKES ABOUT
1¼ CUPS
DRESSING**

MAKING SALAD DRESSINGS IS a great lesson in balancing flavor— they have to hit that sweet spot of just the right amount of acidity, fat, saltiness, sweetness, and umami. Here umami flavors from the Umami Master Sauce and white miso are balanced against the acidity from the lemon, sweetness from the tahini, and sharpness from the sherry vinegar. Use this recipe as a baseline and adjust to suit your taste. You'll find this an easy-to-make dressing that's especially great over mixed greens.

- ½ cup tahini
- ⅓ cup white miso
- ¼ cup water
- 2 tablespoons sherry vinegar
- 1 tablespoon Umami Master Sauce (page 34)
- Juice of 1 lemon
- 4 cups mixed greens (your choice)

1. In a blender, combine the tahini, miso, water, sherry vinegar, master sauce, and lemon juice until the dressing is fully emulsified.

2. Divide the greens among four plates or bowls and drizzle a tablespoon or two of the dressing over each. Toss to coat the leaves, and serve.

3. Leftover dressing can be stored in an airtight jar and refrigerated for up to 3 days.

91

# WARM POTATO SALAD
## WITH YUZU KOSHO DRESSING

**P**OTATO SALADS MOST ALWAYS SUCK. THEY'RE USUALLY bland, underseasoned, chilled too long, mushy . . . yet everyone feels compelled to serve them. It's not hard to make a really great potato salad, though. The key is to make it fresh. And to use a little bit of yuzu kosho dressing, which packs an umami punch. The dressing functions basically as the mustard—albeit a kicked-up one—that's ubiquitous in all potato salad recipes. This potato salad rocks.

- 2 pounds Yukon gold, fingerling, or any other creamy new potatoes, peeled
- Sea salt
- 1 tablespoon olive oil
- 1 large Spanish onion, finely chopped
- 1 recipe Yuzu Kosho Dressing (page 94)
- 3 tablespoons finely chopped fresh chives
- Freshly ground black pepper

1. Place the potatoes in a large saucepan, cover with water by 1 inch, and season generously with salt. Bring to a boil, then reduce the heat to a simmer, and cook until the potatoes are fork tender, 25 to 30 minutes.

2. Meanwhile, in a large skillet over medium-low heat, warm the olive oil. Add the onion and cook, stirring often, until translucent and just tender, 8 to 10 minutes (see Flavor Tip). Transfer the onion to a bowl and let cool.

3. When the potatoes are done, drain and transfer them to a cutting board. When cool enough to handle, smash them with the back of a fork or cut each into ½-inch dice. (Or keep 'em whole—your choice.) Toss the potatoes with the dressing and reserved onion. Add the chives, season with salt and pepper, and toss again. Serve immediately. The acid from the yuzu kosho will break down the potatoes over time, so eat any leftovers within a day.

## SHRIMP SALAD

Instead of potatoes, you can use peeled and deveined shrimp for a fresher take. Poach 2 pounds of shrimp in boiling water for 30 seconds, then pull them out and put them in an ice bath to stop the cooking process. Because shrimp are more delicate than potatoes, you will need only about half of the dressing you would use for the taters. Alternatively, you could serve the dressing on the side as a dip.

### FLAVOR TIP

Do not brown the onion. You're building flavors, with onion at the base. You want to cook it just enough to bring out its sweetness, but not so long that it browns. If it browns, it'll take on a slightly bitter edge that you will taste in the final dish.

# YUZU KOSHO DRESSING

**MAKES ABOUT 1¼ CUPS**

THIS DRESSING IS STRONG RIGHT OFF the bat, which is why it works especially well with ingredients like potatoes that are bland on their own. Use on anything that needs a hit of flavor.

- 1¼ cups mayonnaise (Hellmann's or homemade or anything else you like)
- **3 teaspoons green or red yuzu kosho**
- 1 teaspoon Dijon mustard
- Sea salt and freshly ground black pepper

1. Mix the mayo, yuzu kosho, and Dijon mustard together in a bowl. Season with a pinch of salt and a crack of pepper to taste.

2. Keep refrigerated for up to 1 week.

# AVOCADO AND ROQUEFORT SALAD

SERVES 2

**T**HIS IS A SIMPLE YET sophisticated salad that is super easy to make. Both the ripe avocado and the Roquefort have umami, especially the cheese, so you're taking advantage of Umami Synergy (page 15). Because this salad has so few ingredients, use the best cheese and olive oil you have.

- 1 ripe avocado, halved, pit removed, and peeled
- **3 ounces or more** (depending on how much you love cheese) **good Roquefort, crumbled (about ½ cup)**
- 1 small head butter lettuce, washed and dried
- ½ lemon
- Top-quality extra-virgin olive oil, for drizzling
- Sea salt

1. Fill each avocado half with half of the Roquefort. Set aside.

2. Place the lettuce in a large bowl. Squeeze the lemon over the lettuce and toss. Divide the lettuce between two serving plates or bowls and place a Roquefort-filled avocado half on each. Drizzle olive oil over the avocados and finish with a pinch of salt to taste. Serve.

# FIVE-MINUTE PORK-CONQUERED SALAD

**SERVES 4**

**T**HIS IS ESSENTIALLY A classic spinach and hot bacon salad that won't take you more than 5 minutes to throw together. The cider vinegar is key.

- 6 ounces pork belly, cubed, or 5 bacon slices, chopped
- 1 garlic clove, minced or thinly sliced
- 1 teaspoon honey
- 1 teaspoon Dijon mustard
- ½ cup cider vinegar
- Splash of fish sauce
- Sea salt and freshly ground black pepper
- 2 tablespoons olive oil
- 8 ounces fresh spinach, washed and trimmed of any long stems

1. Crisp up the pork belly or bacon in a heavy pan over medium heat, 6 to 8 minutes, and drain on paper towels, leaving a few tablespoons of the bacon fat in the pan.

2. Drop the heat down to medium-low. Toss the garlic into the pan and toast it up until brown. It'll be quick, about 30 seconds, so keep an eye on it so it doesn't burn.

3. Add the honey, Dijon, cider vinegar, and fish sauce and bring everything to a quick boil. Add a pinch of salt and pepper. Kill the heat and add the olive oil.

4. Place the spinach in a large bowl. Pour the dressing over the greens, folding until all the leaves are lightly coated. Add the pork. There's your pork-conquered salad.

## FOUR-MINUTE PORK-CONQUERED SALAD

Sub in Garlic Confit (page 38) or roasted garlic cloves for the fresh garlic cloves. The garlic's already been cooked, so it's ready to rock right away.

# MAINS

**G**O BIG OR GO HOME. I LOVE TO COOK FAMILY-STYLE FOR large groups and let people attack the platters.

*Highlighted ingredients are staples of the Umami Pantry (page 24).*

and partly because I realized what a perfect vessel burgers are for delivering umami flavors. The beef, the cheese, the caramelized onions, the ketchup: all umami ingredients. From there it was just a matter of perfecting the technique to make the most delicious burger possible.

The most important aspect of the burger is the meat. These are the key tips that will elevate your burger from ordinary to extraordinary:

## NEVER BUY PRE-GROUND MEAT

Pre-ground beef is oxidized and too uniform in texture. Instead buy a nicely marbled cut of beef, like chuck, boneless short ribs (sometimes labeled as chuck tail flap), skirt steak, or hanger steak (the burger will only get better with better beef, so buy the best you can afford). You want a cut that has some fat in it because a patty that's too lean won't hold together during the cooking process and will fall apart. On the other hand, you don't want *too* much fat, either, because a patty that's too fatty will baste instead of sear.

### GRIND THE BEEF AT HOME

Skip the butcher and grind the beef yourself, right before you start cooking. When you grind it yourself, you control the texture of the patty—I personally like a coarse texture—and you minimize how much the meat is handled before you cook it. If you have a meat grinder, use it; if not, don't sweat it. When I was experimenting with the burger that eventually became *the* Umami Burger, all I had was a Cuisinart food processor. I found that cubing and freezing the meat for about 20 minutes made it easier on my processor, and, because the processor generates heat as it works, freezing helped ensure that the beef's delicious, flavorful fat stayed in the meat instead of melting away. It did the trick.

### KEEP IT LOOSE

Resist the temptation to pack the patty. Packing it will make the meat dense and tough; you want it to stay loose so it'll be tender. This loose-pack technique is something I adapted from Heston Blumenthal, the chef at The Fat Duck who also was obsessed with making the perfect burger. He, too, ground the meat himself, but he took care to keep the strands of the meat parallel to each other as they came out of the grinder, before rolling them all up and slicing thin disks to form the patties. (Because the fibers of the meat run in the same direction, his patty is loose and stays juicy.) I found that loosely shaping the meat accomplishes about the same goal in way less time.

### USE A CAST-IRON SKILLET

It retains the heat so the patties will get a nice sear that will contrast with the squishy bun.

One final tip before you start cooking: Disconnect the fire alarm.

# THE UMAMI BURGER

MAKES 1 BURGER

**T**HIS IS IT. THIS IS THE ORIGINAL. *THE* UMAMI BURGER, THE BURGER that I pulled together in my home kitchen with not much more than a few umami-intense ingredients, a cast-iron skillet, and a food processor. This is versatile: If you don't have time to make the Oven-Dried Tomatoes, sub in ripe tomatoes. If you're out of Parmesan cheese, omit the Parmesan cheese crisp. It's your burger. Do it your way.

- 1 cup (4 ounces) grated Parmigiano-Reggiano
- 6 ounces chuck, boneless short ribs, skirt steak, or hanger steak, nicely marbled, about 20% fat, or a combination
- Sea salt and freshly ground black pepper
- 1 tablespoon vegetable oil
- 1 tablespoon unsalted butter
- 1½ ounces fresh shiitake mushrooms, stemmed
- 1 potato bun, split
- Umami Ketchup (page 35)
- Caramelized Onions (page 41)
- 2 slices Oven-Dried Tomatoes (recipe follows) **or ripe tomato**

1. Preheat the oven to 375°F. Line a baking sheet with a Silpat mat or parchment paper.

2. Divide the cheese into neat piles on the baking sheet about 4 inches apart. Flatten the piles with a spatula or the bottom of a cup to form 3-inch rounds.

3. Bake until the rounds are crisp and golden, about 10 minutes, then remove the pan from the oven and cool in the pan for 10 minutes. Using a spatula, carefully transfer the cheese crisps to a rack and let them cool completely before using; you should have 15 to 20 crisps. You'll need only one Parmesan crisp per burger; save the rest for other burgers, or for snacking on later. Store them in an airtight container for up to 3 days. Do not refrigerate.

*continued*

4. While the cheese crisps cool, make the patty. Cube the meat and place it in the freezer for 20 minutes (see page 102). When the meat is cold, place it in your food processor and pulse a few times, just until it's coarsely ground.

5. Place a cast-iron skillet on the highest heat. You want the pan to be wicked hot so you can quickly sear the patty crisp without overcooking the inside.

6. Dump the meat out on a plate and loosely shape it into a flat ball or something close to that general shape. Don't pack the patty—it should barely hold together. Season the patty generously with salt and pepper.

7. Add the oil to the pan, wait a few seconds, then carefully place the patty in the pan; it should crackle and pop right away.

8. Sear the patty for 3 minutes, then flip it over and cook another 3 minutes for a medium-rare burger. Set aside.

9. Lower the flame to medium. Place ½ tablespoon of the butter in a small skillet, then toss in the mushrooms. Sauté until the caps are softened, about 2 minutes. Remove the mushrooms, wipe the skillet clean with a paper towel, throw in the remaining ½ tablespoon butter, and toast both halves of the potato bun cut side down.

10. When the bun is nice and toasted, remove it from the pan and assemble your burger, starting with the ketchup. I like to ketchup both the top and bottom bun, but use as much or as little as you want. Place the patty on the bottom bun and top with the Caramelized Onions, a Parmesan crisp, mushroom caps, tomato slices, and the top bun. Eat. Enjoy.

# OVEN-DRIED TOMATOES

**T**HESE TOMATOES ARE SLICED and dried for several hours—ideally overnight—to really concentrate their umami. Use them on your burgers the next day or, for longer storage, place them in a jar or other container, cover with oil, and keep in the fridge for five to seven days . . . if they last that long!

**MAKES AT LEAST 6 SLICES, DEPENDING ON THE SIZE OF THE TOMATOES AND HOW YOU SLICE THEM**

- 2 medium tomatoes
- 1 tablespoon dark brown sugar
- 1 tablespoon tomato paste
- 1 tablespoon Umami Master Sauce (page 34)
- ½ teaspoon Worcestershire sauce

1. Set your oven to its lowest possible setting. Line a baking sheet with a Silpat mat or parchment paper.

2. Slice the tomatoes as thick or thin as you'd like and place them on the baking sheet. In a small bowl, whisk together the brown sugar, tomato paste, master sauce, and Worcestershire sauce. Brush this mixture onto both sides of the sliced tomatoes.

3. Place the tomatoes in the oven and dry them out, preferably overnight but for at least 6 hours, until shriveled but still juicy.

# SMASHED ONION BURGER

**MAKES 1 BURGER**

**T**HIS SMASHED ONION BURGER IS A RIFF ON WHAT'S KNOWN IN the Midwest as an onion burger. A lot of the flavor here comes through pure technique; it's a simple burger with just a few ingredients. It really doesn't need a lot to dress it up, just the eponymous onion, which is cooked right into the patty, and a thick slice of cheddar cheese. Even the bun doesn't need to be fancy, because its role is to support the meat. An ordinary white supermarket hamburger bun will do, as will a potato bun. Potatoes do have umami, but there's not enough in the bun to over-umamify the burger. Ketchup, on the other hand, might, which is why I omit it.

- **4 ounces chuck, boneless short ribs, skirt steak, or hanger steak, nicely marbled, about 20% fat, or a combination**
- **½ tablespoon Koji-Porcini Resting Sauce** (page 114) or ½ tablespoon unsalted butter
- 1 potato bun or other white hamburger bun, split
- 1 tablespoon corn, canola, or grapeseed oil
- Sea salt and freshly ground black pepper
- **½ small onion, thinly sliced by hand or using a mandoline**
- **Thick slice of cheddar**
- Sweet bread-and-butter pickle slices

1. Cube the meat and stick in the freezer for 20 minutes.

2. Place a cast-iron skillet over high heat for a few minutes. You want this to get as hot as possible.

3. While the skillet preheats, heat the koji resting sauce or the butter in another smaller pan over low heat. Place the bun halves in the pan cut sides down and toast for a few minutes.

4. Next, get your mise en place ready. And get ready. Everything will come together quickly.

5. Transfer the meat from the freezer to your food processor. Pulse a few times until it's coarsely ground, then dump the meat onto a plate. Handling the meat as little as possible, shape it loosely into a patty.

*continued*

6. The skillet should be smoking by now. If it isn't, wait a few more minutes until it is smokin' hot. You don't want to risk burning the onion or the meat once you add them to the pan, so even if your skillet is very well seasoned, add the corn, canola, or grapeseed oil (don't use olive oil, because it'll smoke too fast).

7. Turn on the fan if you've got one.

8. Sprinkle a pinch of salt and pepper on the patty and pick it up with a spatula. Carefully slide the patty into the pan. Once that meat hits the pan, you should hear it sizzling and crackling loudly.

9. Pile the onion on top of the patty. The fat from the meat will start to render, which will baste the patty a little as it cooks. Let the patty cook for about 3 minutes; then flip it over so it's onion side down on the pan.

10. As the second side cooks, you should start to smell the onion. Add the cheese on top, cover, and cook for 2 minutes.

11. Meanwhile, put the toasted bun on a plate and top with the pickles. Remove the patty from the skillet and place it on the bottom half of the bun, onion side down. If you have any sauce or butter left in the skillet, drizzle it over the patty. Top with the other bun half. Cut the burger in half and serve immediately. You should see a rare-ish center and a crispy crust. That contrast is everything.

# KOJI-PORCINI RESTING SAUCE

## MAKES A LITTLE MORE THAN 2 TABLESPOONS

THIS RESTING SAUCE IS FOR THE BURGER BUN (or anything you want to umamify). It's also great with steamed vegetables and will perk up any meat dish. It adds an interesting savory, roasted-mushroomy taste to something that's typically very familiar.

- 8 dried porcini mushrooms
- 2 tablespoons unsalted butter
- ½ teaspoon shio koji

1. Blitz the mushrooms in a spice grinder, blender, or coffee grinder.

2. Place the butter in a small saucepan over low heat. When it just starts to brown and smell a bit nutty, stir in the ground porcinis and shio koji. Once everything combines, remove the pan from the heat and set aside.

3. Use immediately, or place it in a jar or other airtight container and stick it in the fridge for up to a week. Rewarm before using.

# PORT AND STILTON BURGER

**MAKES 1 BURGER**

**R**ESIST THE URGE TO pile any of the usual toppings on this burger— so no lettuce, no tomato, no ketchup. Instead, caramelized onion and Stilton give this burger plenty of flavor, and the port is the only condiment you'll need.

- 1 medium onion, sliced
- 1 star anise
- 2½ teaspoons unsalted butter
- Sea salt
- ¼ cup port
- 6 ounces chuck, boneless short ribs, skirt steak, or hanger steak, nicely marbled, about 20% fat, or a combination
- Freshly ground black pepper
- 2 tablespoons (½ ounce) crumbled Stilton cheese
- Umami Master Dust (page 32)
- 1 potato bun or white hamburger bun, split

1. In a small skillet over very low heat, caramelize the onion slowly (see page 41) with the star anise, 1 teaspoon of the butter, and a pinch of salt, about 45 minutes.

2. Meanwhile, place a small saucepan over medium heat and cook the port until it's reduced to a few tablespoons, 3 to 5 minutes. Set aside.

3. When the onion has caramelized, remove and discard the star anise, add the reduced port, and stir to incorporate.

4. Cube the meat, place it in the freezer for 20 minutes, then pulse it a few times in a food processor until it looks ground but still chunky. Form by hand or, for a neater presentation, in a 4-inch ring mold, being careful not to pack it tightly—you want it to be loose and just barely formed. Season the patty generously with salt and pepper.

5. Heat a cast-iron griddle or skillet over high heat. While it heats up, melt the remaining 1½ teaspoons butter in a small pan over low heat. Toast the buns, cut side down, for a few minutes, then set aside.

6. When the griddle is very hot, place the patty on it, cover with a roasting pan, and cook over medium-high heat for 4 minutes, until it's very crusty. Flip the patty and cook, covered, for 2 minutes longer. Then top with the Stilton and cook, uncovered, for 1 minute.

7. Transfer the patty to a plate and sprinkle on a pinch of the master dust. Let the patty rest for 2 minutes before setting it on the bottom half of the hamburger bun. Pile the onion onto the patty, then top with the other bun half. Serve.

# VEGGIE BURGER

MAKES 2
BURGERS

- 4 dried porcini mushrooms
- ¼ cup medium-dry sherry, like amontillado
- 1 tablespoon white miso
- Splash of Umami Master Sauce (page 34)
- 2 large egg yolks
- ½ cup panko bread crumbs or textured vegetable protein (see headnote)
- 2 tablespoons toasted or regular sesame oil
- 1 cup stemmed and sliced fresh shiitake mushrooms
- Sea salt and freshly ground black pepper
- 2 potato buns or white hamburger buns, split
- 1 tablespoon Koji-Porcini Resting Sauce (page 114) or unsalted butter

. . . . . . . . . . .

**OPTIONAL CONDIMENTS AND TOPPINGS**

- Mayonnaise
- Ketchup
- Mustard

**I** **USE MUSHROOMS AS THE PRIMARY** component for my veggie burger and infuse them with miso, a bit of Umami Master Sauce, and egg yolks—all from the Umami Pantry—to bump up the flavor even more.

Because the patties need a few hours to set, prep them the night before and they'll be ready to go when it's time to start cooking.

Note: Textured vegetable protein (TVP), also sold as textured soy protein, is available at Whole Foods, health food stores, or online at Amazon.

1. Place the dried porcinis, sherry, miso, and master sauce in a small saucepan. Set the heat to medium-low and simmer until the liquid is almost gone, rehydrating the mushrooms, about 10 minutes.

2. Remove the pan from the heat, cool, then add the egg yolks and panko (or textured vegetable protein). Pulse the mixture in a food processor to incorporate. Set aside.

3. Heat a large skillet over high heat for a few minutes—you want it to get superhot. Add 1 tablespoon of the sesame oil, wait a minute, then throw in the shiitakes, being careful not to crowd the mushrooms. Season with salt and pepper, and sauté until they're nicely caramelized, about 6 minutes. Remove the mushrooms to a large bowl and let cool.

4. When the mushrooms have cooled, add the egg yolk mixture and stir to incorporate. I use a 3-inch ring mold to press out the patties, but if you don't have a mold, free-form 2 patties with your hands. Be sure to pack the patties fairly tight so they don't fall apart when you cook them. Refrigerate the patties at least 6 hours or overnight, to set.

5. You can also place the patties side by side on a baking sheet or dish and stick them in the freezer; when they're frozen, place the patties in an airtight bag and keep them in the freezer for up to 2 months. Thaw completely before cooking.

6. When you're ready to cook, heat a large skillet over medium-high heat with the remaining tablespoon of sesame oil and sauté the patties for 3 minutes on each side. Remove the patties and set aside. Place the Koji-Porcini Resting Sauce or butter in the pan and place the buns cut side down in the pan for a few minutes, just until they're toasted and warmed through.

7. Place the patties in the buns and serve with the condiments and toppings of your choice.

**I**F YOU'VE NEVER GRILLED MUCH BEFORE, THIS IS A great way to start. Honestly, I was a crappy grill cook when I first started, so don't give up if your first few pizzas don't turn out as perfect as you'd like them to. They'll still be delicious! You don't even need a fancy setup; a $100 Weber kettle grill will do, especially if it has a cast-iron grill that keeps the heat.

What you absolutely *don't* want is a gas grill. A gas grill will not get hot enough, and without that super-high heat, your pizza will cook through (slowly) before it chars. And, unlike wood, gas adds zero flavor.

# PIZZA DOUGH
## AND BASIC GRILLING METHOD

**MAKES ENOUGH DOUGH FOR FOUR 8-INCH PIZZAS**

THE DOUGH I MAKE IS BASED ON THE VERSION MADE AT AL FORNO, the Providence restaurant that became known for grilling pizza over charcoal, though I've added significantly more water to increase the overall hydration of the dough. If you can, start on the dough the night before you plan to grill; the dough will rise overnight in your fridge and develop great flavor as it ferments, giving you a slightly nutty, slightly tangy crust.

The dough should be rolled out thin. When you grill it, you'll cook one side, flip it, and cook the other side while you put the toppings on. For the toppings, remember the crust is thin, so don't load up *too* much. Instead, use a few simple, flavorful ingredients like prosciutto, ripe tomatoes, caramelized onions, and cheese. Note that meat toppings like sausage should be cooked, or 99 percent cooked, before putting them on the pizzas, because there won't be any time to cook them otherwise.

Above all, work quickly. Once the dough is over the fire, everything happens superfast. You'll be rewarded for your spontaneity.

* 1 tablespoon extra-virgin olive oil, plus more for brushing
* 2 cups warm water
* Pinch of sugar or ½ teaspoon honey
* 1 packet (2½ teaspoons) active dry yeast
* ¼ cup fine-ground white cornmeal
* 3 tablespoons whole-wheat flour
* 2¼ teaspoons salt
* 3 cups unbleached all-purpose flour, plus more for dusting
* Oil from Garlic Confit (page 38) or canola oil, for brushing

*continued*

1. A few hours or the day before you plan to grill the pizzas, make the dough. Brush a large bowl with olive oil and set aside.

2. In another large bowl, pour in 1 cup of the warm water and the sugar or honey. Add the yeast and give it a good stir to dissolve; you're waking up the yeast to get it going. You'll know it's active when the yeast dissolves and starts to foam. (If it doesn't foam, the water may have been too hot and killed the yeast, or your pack of yeast may have been too old.)

3. After 5 minutes, add the cornmeal, whole-wheat flour, the tablespoon of olive oil, and the salt to the yeast and stir everything together with a spoon. Slowly stir in ¼ cup of the all-purpose flour, then a few tablespoons from the remaining cup of water; continue adding the flour and the water, in turns, until everything is incorporated and the dough is stiff yet moist.

4. Turn the dough out onto a floured surface. Time for some elbow grease. Knead the dough until it's smooth and shiny, a few minutes. The dough will be sticky; use a light, quick touch. If the dough is still too sticky for you to handle, add a little more all-purpose flour to help you along.

5. When the dough is kneaded, transfer it to the oiled bowl. Brush the top of the dough with olive oil to prevent a skin from forming and cover with plastic wrap. You can put it in the fridge to rise overnight or, if you're making the pizza later on in the day, let it rise in a warm place, away from drafts, until doubled in size. How long it takes depends on how warm your place is; mine usually doubles in 1½ to 2 hours.

6. When the dough has doubled, remove the plastic wrap and punch it down. Reflour your kneading surface, and then knead the dough until it's again smooth and shiny. Reoil the bowl, place the dough back in it, cover, and let the dough rise again for about 40 minutes.

7.  Punch down the dough one last time, then pull it onto a floured surface. Divide the dough into 4 equal pieces and roll them out (shape isn't super important—squares, circles, do whatever you like). Whatever the shape, make it about ¼ inch thick so it'll cook quickly on the grill.

8.  Start the grill: Get your grill ready. You can use a chimney smoker to start it up. Be sure to use hardwood charcoal, which will burn hot (see Flavor Tip). Don't use lighter fluid, and don't use a gas grill if you can avoid it: Gas won't get hot enough, and, unlike hardwood, gas imparts no flavor. Oil the grate with the oil from Garlic Confit, for extra flavor, or canola oil.

9.  Place your hand a few inches above the grill. When you can only keep it there for two seconds before having to snatch your hand away, the grill is hot enough to cook pizza.

10. While you're waiting for the grill to come to temp, bring out the dough and set up your toppings assembly line–style. Have platters ready to plate the pizza.

11. Grill the pizza: Working with one crust at a time, carefully slide the dough onto the grill and brush garlic confit oil or canola oil on the dough. The surface will bubble as it cooks. Using tongs, check the underside. When you see grill marks there (see Flavor Tip), about 2 minutes, flip the dough and move it to the cooler side of the grill.

12. Add your toppings, bring the pizza back over the flame, cover to melt any cheese you're using, and cook for just a minute or two more. Repeat with the remaining dough. Serve.

## PITA BREAD

The dough also makes a great pita bread. Roll out the dough ⅛ inch thick and cook it in a cast-iron skillet over high heat on your stovetop, about 3 minutes per side. It will be golden, with a few super-toasty or charred spots on each side.

---

### FLAVOR TIPS

Use a variety of hardwood, like cedar, mesquite, and applewood, for your grill. The wet dough will absorb those subtle, smoky flavors.

Don't be afraid to let your pizza char a little. That's the Maillard reaction at work and will give your pie extra character and flavor.

# GRILLED TRICOLOR PIZZA

**M**Y TRICOLOR PIZZA HAS three cheeses and three sauces. Each has a ton of flavor, and together they give you three colorful layers: the red from the tomato sauce, the green from a smooth basil puree, and the white from a combination of ricotta, Burrata, and Pecorino. (You can also use any other soft cheeses that will melt properly, like mozzarella and fontina.) The flavors complement each other well, and it's as pretty as it is delicious.

Note: You can also use any one of the sauces as a building block for other pizzas, or use them as dips for crusty bread.

- ◆ **1 recipe Pizza Dough** (page 121)
- ◆ **Olive oil**
- ◆ **1 cup Umami-Minded Tomato Sauce** (page 128)
- ◆ **1 recipe Basil Puree** (page 129)
- ◆ **1 recipe Parmesan Fonduta** (page 134)
- ◆ **1 cup (8 ounces) ricotta**
- ◆ **8 ounces (2 balls) Burrata, torn into small and large pieces**
- ◆ **Pecorino, for grating**

**MAKES FOUR 8-INCH PIZZAS**

1. Roll out the dough, brush your grill grate with some olive oil, and get your first pizza going on the grill. When you flip the dough, move it over to the cooler part of the grill and layer on the three sauces—the Umami-Minded Tomato Sauce, Basil Puree, and Parmesan Fonduta—one at a time. How you want to place these sauces on the pizza is up to you and your artistic intuition: You can layer them directly on top of one another or splatter them on as you see fit. Then add dollops of the ricotta and Burrata.

2. Move the pizza back to the hot part of the grill and close the lid. After 2 minutes, lift the lid; the cheese should be melted and the dough should be crisp and brown with a few air bubbles here and there, with flecks of char. Carefully slide the pizza onto a pizza peel or platter. Repeat with the remaining dough. Shower each pizza with a grating of fresh Pecorino and serve.

# UMAMI-MINDED TOMATO SAUCE

**F**OR AN UMAMI-INFUSED TAKE on the traditional Italian tomato sauce, try my version. I stick with tradition by starting with onion and garlic and adding in tomatoes and basil, but then veer away and incorporate a few decidedly un-Italian ingredients: soy sauce, fish sauce, and Umami Master Sauce. I then puree the sauce at the end for a uniform texture that belies its complex flavors. It will taste great with most toppings; use it as a foundational layer for any pizza or flatbread you make, or in the Umami Stromboli (page 79).

## MAKES 3 CUPS

- 1 cup water
- 4 dried porcini mushrooms
- 2 tablespoons extra-virgin olive oil
- 2 garlic cloves, sliced
- 1 small onion or 2 shallots, finely chopped
- 1 (28-ounce) can San Marzano–style plum tomatoes or other top-quality canned tomatoes
- ½ teaspoon soy sauce, preferably Japanese
- Dash of fish sauce
- Dash of shio koji
- ½ teaspoon red yuzu kosho
- ½ teaspoon Umami Master Sauce (page 34)
- ½ teaspoon honey
- 6 fresh basil leaves

1. In a small saucepan over low heat, warm the water. Turn off the heat and add the dried porcinis. Soak the mushrooms until they're completely rehydrated, 20 to 30 minutes. Strain the water through a fine-mesh sieve or coffee filter; discard any grit or dirt and set the water aside with the mushrooms.

2. Meanwhile, heat the olive oil in a large saucepan or Dutch oven over medium-low heat. When the oil ripples, add the garlic and onion (or shallots) and sauté until the garlic is fragrant and the onion is translucent, about 5 minutes.

3. Add the plum tomatoes, soy sauce, fish sauce, shio koji, red yuzu kosho, master sauce, honey, and the soaked mushrooms and their water. Stir, bring to a boil, then turn the heat down to very low. Simmer the sauce for 1 hour, or until the tomatoes have broken down a bit and everything is nice and soft. Stir in the basil leaves. Remove from the heat, cool, transfer the sauce to a blender, and puree until smooth.

4. Any leftovers can be refrigerated and used within 3 days. The sauce also will freeze well. Reheat as needed.

## FASTER BOLOGNESE SAUCE

Traditionally, meat sauce, meat ragu, and Bolognese (all the same thing) cook very slowly, but I found a good way to hack it quickly. If you have leftover braised beef, or Sweet and Savory Brisket (page 74), add chunks of that straight from the fridge into the pureed Umami-Minded Tomato Sauce and simmer everything for an hour. The braised meat will fall apart into shreds, thickening the sauce. Serve over any pasta.

# BASIL PUREE

**MAKES 1 CUP**

**H**ERE IS A SIMPLE, DELICIOUS BASE FOR any pizza topped with vegetables or meat. Use what you need for your pizza, then hang on to the leftovers and use them as a dipping sauce for the crust.

- 2 cups (4 ounces) tightly packed fresh basil
- 1 garlic clove, peeled
- ½ cup olive oil, plus more if needed
- ½ teaspoon sea salt

1. Fill a large bowl with iced water. Set aside.

2. Set a large saucepan of water over high heat and bring it almost to a boil—you should just start to see big bubbles on the surface of the water. At that point, drop in the basil and blanch it for 15 seconds. Pull it out and immediately drop it into the bowl of iced water and remove. This process will set the color so the basil stays bright green.

3. Transfer the basil to a blender with the garlic clove and oil and puree, adding more oil if needed to liquefy fully. Season with the salt.

4. Jar any leftovers and refrigerate; it'll keep for a few days.

# GRILLED TARTE FLAMBÉE

**MAKES FOUR 8-INCH PIZZAS**

TOOK THE CLASSIC TARTE FLAMBÉE, WHERE THE DOUGH IS rolled out thin and topped with very simple—but excellent—ingredients, including cheese, bacon, and onions, and bumped up the umami with Parmesan Fonduta and Caramelized Onions.

---

- **Smoked bacon, pancetta, or guanciale**
- **1 recipe Pizza Dough** (page 121)
- **Oil from Garlic Confit** (page 38) **or canola oil, for brushing**
- **1 cup crème fraîche**
- **1 recipe Parmesan Fonduta** (page 134)
- **1 cup (8 ounces) cow's milk or sheep's milk ricotta**
- **Caramelized Onions** (page 41)

1. If you're using bacon or pancetta, cook it before you bring it out to the grill. Guanciale is cured, so if you're using that, just sauté it for a minute or two until it's warmed through before using it as a pizza topping.

2. Roll out the dough, brush your grill grate with the garlic confit oil or canola oil, and get ready—the pizzas cook fast. Place one pizza on the grill and cook for 2 minutes, then brush on some oil, flip it over, and move it to the cooler side of the grill. Add the toppings: Spread ¼ cup of the crème fraîche on the pizza, then a quarter of the Parmesan Fonduta. Dot the surface with a quarter of the ricotta and add as much Caramelized Onions and meat as you like.

3. Move the pizza back over the direct heat and close the lid. This is a flambée, so let the pizza smoke for about 3 minutes.

4. Lift the lid. The cheese should be melted and the crust should be crispy with flecks of char here and there, but if it hasn't yet reached that point, put the lid back on for another minute and then check it again. When it's done, remove the pizza, repeat with the remaining dough, and serve.

it is used sparingly—just to finish a bowl of pasta or salad. But awesome things happen when the cheese is the main ingredient, as in this fonduta.

It goes well with something as simple as cubes of crusty bread and roasted fingerling potatoes—or with almost any vegetable—and when cooled it's perfect as a topping for pizza or in lasagna.

Because this dish is all about the Parmesan, use the best you can afford to buy. Be sure to grate it finely or it won't melt properly. For a luxurious bump in flavor, add truffle butter, which you can order through Truffle Brothers or on Amazon (see Sources, page 248).

- ◆ **4 fresh sage leaves**
- ◆ **1 cup heavy cream**
- ◆ **2 large egg yolks**
- ◆ **1 cup finely grated Parmigiano-Reggiano** (see headnote)
- ◆ **Black or white truffle butter** (optional; see Sources, page 248)
- ◆ **Freshly ground white pepper** (optional)

................

FOR DIPPING

- ◆ **1 baguette, torn into pieces or cut into cubes**
- ◆ **Roasted fingerling potatoes**
- ◆ **Roasted vegetables** (see Caramelized Root Vegetables, page 208)

1. Chiffonade the sage by stacking the leaves and rolling them lengthwise. Starting at one end of the roll, slice the leaves crosswise so you end up with a neat pile of ribbons.

2. Heat the cream in a small saucepan over medium heat and drop in the sage. Once the cream starts to boil, pull the pan off the heat and carefully press the sage leaves against the inside of the pot using the back of a spoon (see Flavor Tip). Give the cream one more swirl.

3. Strain the cream, then pour it back into the pan over low heat. Whisk in the yolks and cheese. Add the truffle butter, if you're using it. As the egg combines with the cream and the cheese melts, the fonduta will thicken; continue whisking for a few minutes more, until everything is well combined. Taste. If you want, finish with a few grinds of pepper. Transfer to a fondue pot or a pretty bowl, alongside the bread, potatoes, and vegetables so your guests can pick and dip at their leisure.

FLAVOR TIP

Pressing the sage will release its valuable oils into the cream, giving the fonduta an extra pop of flavor.

# MIDNIGHT GARLIC NOODLES

**MAKES 2 BOWLS OF NOODLES**

**T**HE NAME SAYS IT ALL. WHIP UP THESE GARLICKY NOODLES with the leftovers in your fridge for a fast, delicious late-night snack. Everything about this dish is a lesson in improvising with what you have. The Garlic Confit pairs nicely with the Burnt Miso, but fresh garlic will also work, as will roasted garlic. You can omit the miso from the puree if you're out; even with just garlic and noodles, this is a satisfying quick meal.

One thing you will want to do is keep any leftover sauce. It'll last up to a week in the fridge and will taste good on most everything. It's even good right off of the spoon—it's my peanut butter.

- Sea salt if using Italian pasta
- **12 ounces whatever noodles you have in your pantry** (I like the fresh ramen from the Asian market or a good dried Italian pasta.)
- **2 tablespoons Burnt Miso** (page 47)
- **½ teaspoon shio koji**
- **10 to 15 cloves Garlic Confit** (page 38), **depending on how garlicky you like your noodles**
- **2 tablespoons oil from Garlic Confit** (page 38) **or olive oil**
- **1 tablespoon unsalted butter**
- **Freshly ground black pepper**
- **Fleur de sel** (optional)
- **Parmigiano-Reggiano** (optional)

1. Bring a large saucepan of water to a boil—don't forget to salt the water if you're using Italian pasta—and cook the noodles according to the directions on the package.

2. While the noodles boil, make the garlic-miso sauce. Place the Burnt Miso, shio koji, Garlic Confit, and 1 tablespoon of oil in a blender or food processor and puree until smooth. Add the butter and scoop out and add ¼ cup pasta water and puree again. It'll thin out and become more sauce-like, which is exactly what you want.

3. Place a large skillet over low heat and add the remaining tablespoon of oil and the garlic-miso sauce. When the noodles are just about done, drain them or use tongs to transfer them from the saucepan directly into the skillet. Stir to combine, and finish with the pepper.

4. Taste for seasoning. If the noodles need a kick of salt, add a pinch of fleur de sel and top with freshly grated Parmesan.

# PASTA WITH ROASTED HEIRLOOM TOMATO SAUCE

SERVES 4

**T**HIS IS YOUR BASIC SPAGHETTI-AND-TOMATO-SAUCE RECIPE KICKED up with some Umami Master Dust, Umami Master Sauce, anchovy, and soy sauce. I use heirloom tomatoes here, which are generally at their flavor peak in the late summer, and roast them to maximize their umami. While this is best as a summer dish because of the heirlooms, Roma tomatoes will do, too. Regardless, don't worry about choosing pristine tomatoes for this sauce. Because the tomatoes cook down completely, it's a good chance to use any ugly and overripe tomatoes you have sitting around or see at the market. If you have the Umami Master Sauce and Master Dust ready to go, dinner will come together in about half an hour—and will look so simple that even your kids will love it.

Note: You can easily make the sauce vegetarian-friendly. Just omit the anchovy.

## TOMATO SAUCE

- **3 pounds heirloom tomatoes**
- **Sea salt and freshly ground black pepper**
- **A few sprigs thyme**
- **Oil from Garlic Confit** (page 38) **or extra-virgin olive oil**
- **1 teaspoon unsalted butter**
- **1 tablespoon Umami Master Sauce** (page 34)
- **1 tablespoon Umami Master Dust** (page 32)
- **1 tablespoon tomato paste**
- **1 anchovy fillet, rinsed and chopped**
- **1 tablespoon white or dark soy sauce**
- **Chili oil or red pepper flakes** (optional)
- **1 pound fresh or dried Italian pasta, preferably an egg pasta like tagliatelle**

## FOR SERVING

- **1 cup ricotta,** **Burrata, or fresh mozzarella cheese, or a mix of all three**
- **1 cup Parmesan Bread Crumbs** (page 48), **toasted**
- **Freshly grated Parmigiano-Reggiano**
- **Fresh chives, chopped** (optional)

*continued*

1. **MAKE THE SAUCE:** Preheat the oven to 325°F.

2. Quarter the tomatoes and place them in a large cast-iron skillet. Season them with salt and pepper and the thyme sprigs, then spoon in a few tablespoons of Garlic Confit oil or extra-virgin olive oil. You need enough oil to coat the tomatoes generously, so add more if you need to. Roast the tomatoes for about an hour, until their skins shrivel and they collapse upon themselves.

3. Next make the base for the tomato sauce. In a medium saucepan over low heat, place 1 tablespoon of oil, the butter, master sauce, master dust, tomato paste, anchovy, and soy sauce. Stir to combine and cook for 5 minutes, until slightly thickened. Turn off the heat and set aside until the tomatoes are done.

4. When the tomatoes have roasted, take them out of the oven. The tomatoes will have released a lot of liquid; carefully add that liquid to the tomato base and stir. Then place the base over very low heat and let simmer.

5. Remove and discard the skins from the tomatoes (you should be able to pull them off easily). Discard the thyme sprigs.

6. Add the tomatoes to the tomato base and crush them slightly with a spoon. Let the sauce continue to simmer until it reduces by about half and thickens, about 15 minutes.

7. When the sauce is about done, spice it up with a drizzle of chili oil or a pinch of red pepper flakes if you'd like, then take the pot off the heat and set it aside while you make the pasta (see Flavor Tip).

8. Bring a large pot of salted water to a boil—the water should taste like the ocean: salty!—and cook the pasta according to the package's directions.

9. Before you drain the pasta, take 3 teaspoons of the pasta water and add to the tomato sauce. The salt from the water will add a little extra seasoning, and the starch from the pasta will help re-emulsify the sauce and add body.

10. To serve, portion the pasta into bowls. Ladle the sauce into each and follow with a generous spoonful of ricotta, Burrata, or mozzarella and a sprinkle of the Parmesan Bread Crumbs. Finish with the Parmesan cheese to taste and fresh chives, if desired. Dig in.

---

**FLAVOR TIP**

I start boiling the pasta after I've made the sauce, so the sauce will have cooled down to a perfect temperature by the time the noodles are al dente. That way you can taste the sauce's multiple layers of flavor.

# Is It Authentic?

**A**UTHENTICITY DOESN'T automatically make a dish better. I have had crappy "authentic" dishes in their mother countries. By the same token, if a dish is deemed inauthentic it doesn't necessarily mean it's bad. I have had modernist-inspired re-creations and deconstructions of classic ideas using new cooking equipment that struck me as improvements upon the originals.

I can see why people use authenticity as a guide, though, because we need two decidedly different approaches when visiting restaurants these days: Is this restaurant a good example of tradition or does it succeed on its own terms? Modernist restaurants cannot be judged the same way as classic bistros, and that's why we need educated expectations.

Authenticity might seem like an absolute ideal when building your palate, but it's often confused with finding our favorite version of a dish or having a memorable palate experience. Frequently when we call a dish authentic, we really just mean it's traditional—a classic. Those dishes, those classics that keep people coming back and back and back, are proven successful combinations of flavors.

Classic dishes are concepts that work, but they're not set in stone.

By all means, learn the classics and use them to help you master cooking techniques, but don't be afraid to do your own thing with them. As Paul Bertolli, the chef of the Oakland restaurant Oliveto, wrote in his book *Cooking by Hand*, we need to "clean the fresco." In other words, take the dish back to its origins, see what purpose the dish served back then, and appreciate it on its own, not just the rote process it may have become. When I started playing around with burgers, for example, I first went back to the basics. I thought about what made burgers at places like In-N-Out so satisfying in the first place: It's the charred patty, the melted cheese, the caramelized onions, sure. But then I pushed the boundaries and nudged the burger toward the future instead of looking back. Food from the soul of the person feeding you is the real authentic food, however common or uncommon.

Food evolves. Art evolves. I love classic renditions of pasta Bolognese, but I'd love to see how some of the best chefs in the world play with the dish after mastering it. I wouldn't be surprised if the best version of pasta Bolognese isn't a traditional version at all: It could be the one someone in Bologna is experimenting with using modern techniques right now. Take, for example, my Umami-Minded Tomato Sauce (page 128). It is not authentic Italian in the least, but it's still very delicious.

# WHITE ON WHITE PASTA

SERVES 4

**L**OTS OF FLAVOR COMES UNEXPECTEDLY from this improvised recipe. I use dried pasta (my favorite) and a larger shape, like conchiglioni, cencioni, orecchiette, or torchietti. My preferred dried pastas come from Rustichella d'Abruzzo, which you can find on Amazon. Amazon also sells truffle butter, which is an option for this recipe.

- Sea salt
- 1 pound dried pasta
  (see headnote)
- 2 tablespoons white truffle butter (see headnote)
  or unsalted butter
- 2 tablespoons oil from Garlic Confit (page 38), garlic oil, or extra-virgin olive oil
- ¾ cup (6 ounces) ricotta
- Freshly ground black pepper
- Freshly grated Parmigiano-Reggiano, for serving

1. Bring a large pot of salted water to a boil and cook the pasta according to the directions on the package until al dente. Drain, reserving a few tablespoons of the pasta water.

2. To the now-empty pasta pot, add the butter and oil. Add the reserved pasta water and whisk to emulsify. Add the pasta and stir. Portion the pasta onto plates, adding dabs of fresh ricotta. Season with salt, pepper, and grated Parmesan. Serve. Enjoy.

# AL DENTE
# MAC AND CHEESE

**I LIKE PASTA TO BE AL DENTE, AND NO PASTA DISH IS MUSHIER** than mac and cheese. This is an adult version with a high crust-to-pasta ratio and umami-filled cheese.

You know how some cheeses separate into an oily liquid and blocks of solids as they melt? The separation occurs because of what happens when the proteins in the cheeses are exposed to high heat for too long. At room temp the fat and the liquid in the cheese are in a perfect, emulsified state. Once you add heat, the proteins that keep the emulsification going start to weaken. Eventually the proteins give way altogether and the cheese separates. Sodium citrate prevents that from happening by keeping everything emulsified and smooth. You can get sodium citrate on Amazon; you can also omit it, though the cheese won't end up quite as smooth.

- 2 cups whole milk
- Sea salt
- 12 ounces hard cheese (I use caciocavallo, an Italian cow's or sheep's milk cheese; aged Gouda, cheddar, Comté, Manchego, and Gruyère are good substitutes) or a mix of them, grated
- 1 cup (4 ounces) grated Parmigiano-Reggiano
- 2 tablespoons unsalted butter
- Pinch of fresh grated nutmeg
- 3 teaspoons sodium citrate (optional; see headnote)
- 1 pound dried pasta (I use a large fusilli)
- ½ cup Parmesan Bread Crumbs (page 48), untoasted

1. Heat the milk in a large saucepan over low heat. Add 1 teaspoon of salt, the grated cheeses, butter, and nutmeg. Stir until melted. Add the sodium citrate, if using. Cool for 5 minutes, then blend on low in a blender.

2. Bring a large pot of salted water to a boil. Add the pasta and cook according to the directions on the package until al dente. Drain.

3. Preheat the broiler.

4. Return the pasta to the now-empty pot and add enough of the cheese sauce to coat it thickly. Pour into a shallow 9-by-13-inch casserole or gratin dish. Add the remaining sauce. Top with the bread crumbs.

5. Put under the broiler for about 3 minutes, or until brown. Serve.

# VEAL MARSALA PASTA

**SERVES 4**

**T**RADITIONALLY THE sauce for veal Marsala pasta is made with mushrooms, Marsala wine, and stock. I take braising liquid from leftover Osso Buco and super-flavorful dried mushrooms to form the base of the sauce. There are two textures of veal going on here: the scaloppine and the falling-apart-tender veal from the Osso Buco.

This will *not* taste like leftovers!

- 1 cup water
- 2 ounces dried morels or other dried mushrooms
- Sea salt
- 12 ounces dried pappardelle or other wide egg pasta
- Leftover Osso Buco (page 176) or other braised veal
- 1 tablespoon extra-virgin olive oil
- 1 tablespoon bacon, finely chopped
- 8 ounces sliced fresh mushrooms, like oyster or stemmed shiitake mushrooms
- 4 veal scaloppine (cutlets), about 3 ounces each
- Freshly ground black pepper
- ¼ cup Marsala wine
- Parmigiano-Reggiano, for serving

1. In a small saucepan over low heat, warm the water. Turn off the heat and add the dried mushrooms. Soak the mushrooms until they're completely rehydrated, 20 to 30 minutes. Strain the water through a fine-mesh sieve or coffee filter; discard any grit or dirt and set the water aside with the mushrooms.

2. When the mushrooms have nearly rehydrated, start the pasta. Bring a large pot of salted water to a boil. Add the pasta and cook according to the directions on the package until al dente. Drain.

3. Preheat the broiler.

4. Strain the leftover Osso Buco and set aside the meat and ¼ cup of the liquid. Taste it—it will probably be salty. Keep that in mind as you season the other components of the dish.

5. In a large cast-iron skillet over high heat, add the olive oil, then the bacon. Sauté until just barely cooked, a few minutes.

6. Add the fresh mushrooms to the pan. Don't touch them just yet—let them crisp and do their thing for a minute. When they've started to brown nicely, sauté until they're browned all over, 3 to 5 minutes. Add the rehydrated mushrooms (hold on to the liquid—you'll use it in a second) and the veal from the Osso Buco and stir for 2 minutes to warm up the veal, breaking up the meat with a spoon.

7. Meanwhile, season both sides of the veal scaloppine with a pinch of salt and pepper. Nudge the mushrooms and bacon to one side of the pan and add the scaloppine. Cook each side just long enough for it to get some color, 1 to 2 minutes per side.

8. Now hit the pan with the Marsala. Wait a minute for the wine to reduce (see Flavor Tip), then pour the reserved ¼ cup of strained osso buco liquid and the liquid from the rehydrated mushrooms into the pan.

9. Transfer the pan to the broiler for 1 minute to give color to the veal, then place it back on the stove with the heat reduced to medium.

10. Add the drained pasta to the pan. Season, if needed, with salt and pepper. Grate the Parmesan directly on top. Serve.

---

### FLAVOR TIP

Always put in the alcohol before the stock. You want the flavor of the Marsala, not the alcohol, in your sauce, so boil off the alcohol before combining it with the braising liquid.

# FUNKY, PORKY RAGU

**SERVES 4**

COTECHINO IS A FRESH PORK SAUSAGE, ALMOST LIKE AN Italian pâté, traditionally eaten with lentils and mashed potatoes on New Year's Day. I use it here as the main component of a super-funky ragu, which is great with pasta or Traditional Potato Gnocchi (page 148). Like many sauces, this ragu doesn't need to be made to order—it's even better the next day, after the flavors have had a night in the fridge to integrate.

I get canned cherry tomatoes and cotechino from the Truffle Brothers (see Sources, page 248). If you can't find canned cherry tomatoes, swap them out for whole peeled tomatoes, preferably from San Marzano (the can's label should have its place of origin). And instead of the cotechino, you can use 12 ounces of mixed salamis, diced, or fresh chorizo.

- 12 ounces cotechino, chopped (see headnote), or a mix of diced salami or fresh chorizo
- 1 ounce chopped guanciale
- 2 tablespoons extra-virgin olive oil, plus more for garnish
- 1 small onion, minced
- Sea salt and freshly ground black pepper
- 1 garlic clove, minced
- 1 carrot, coarsely grated
- Half of a 14-ounce can cherry tomatoes or whole peeled tomatoes, drained

- ½ cup dry white wine
- 2 tablespoons tomato paste
- 1 bay leaf
- 1 teaspoon sugar
- 1½ cups chicken stock
- 16 ounces high-quality Italian pasta (see Sources, page 248) or 1 recipe Traditional Potato Gnocchi (page 148)
- ¼ cup freshly grated Parmigiano-Reggiano, plus more for garnish
- 2 sprigs fresh Mexican oregano
- 1 teaspoon chili oil (optional)

1. In a large skillet, cook the cotechino or other sausage and the guanciale over medium heat, breaking up any clumps, until the meats begin to brown, 8 to 10 minutes. Scrape the meats onto a plate. Drain the fat from the skillet, then add the 2 tablespoons of oil and the onion. Season with a generous pinch of salt and pepper and cook until the onion is translucent, 8 to 10 minutes. Add the garlic and cook for another 2 minutes. Add the carrot and cook, stirring, until softened, about 2 minutes. Still over the heat, add the tomatoes and break them up with a wooden spoon.

2. Add the wine and stir, scraping up any browned bits from the pan. Cook until the wine has reduced by two-thirds, about 3 minutes. Return the meats to the skillet. Add the tomato paste, bay leaf, sugar, and chicken stock. Bring the sauce to a boil, then simmer over medium-low heat, stirring, until reduced by half, about 45 minutes. Cool and refrigerate, covered, overnight to marry the flavors.

3. When ready to serve, bring a large pot of salted water to a boil. Add the pasta and cook according to the directions on the package until al dente. Drain. If using the gnocchi, cook according to the instructions in the recipe.

4. Meanwhile, place the refrigerated ragu over low heat. Stir in the ¼ cup of cheese and the oregano and season again with salt and pepper. Add the teaspoon of chili oil if you're using it, and rewarm everything, being careful not to boil the ragu. Just before serving, remove the oregano and bay leaf.

5. You can place all the pasta or gnocchi in a large serving bowl with the sauce ladled on top and serve it family-style, or divide the pasta and sauce among four bowls. Either way, garnish with grated Parmesan, drizzle with olive oil, and season with a tiny amount of salt and pepper.

# TRADITIONAL
# POTATO GNOCCHI

**SERVES 4 TO 6**

**P**OTATO GNOCCHI HAS A REPUTATION FOR BEING DENSE AND HEAVY, but it should be light and ethereal. You can easily make pillowy gnocchi at home by baking the potatoes until they're fork tender. *Fork* tender: Use a fork, not a knife, to check the potatoes, as a knife's sharp blade may be misleading. Then use a potato ricer or food mill to mash the potatoes; in a pinch, a fork and some elbow grease will do, too. Whatever you do, don't use a food processor, because that will give you a gummy starch bomb.

After that it's just a matter of using a light touch to make the dough, incorporating as little flour as possible. Aside from the Yukon gold potatoes' natural buttery flavor, the gnocchi itself will be a little plain. It's perfect when combined with an assertive sauce like Funky, Porky Ragu (page 146). If you want to incorporate more umami into the basic gnocchi, out the Yukon golds for a blander potato like a Russet (Idaho) and substitute the type 0 flour with truffle flour (see Sources, page 248).

Note: The protein in flour helps form the gluten in the dough. In turn, the strength of the gluten network directly affects the structure of the final product. To make a light, airy cake, for example, you'd want to use cake flour, which has about 7 percent protein content. For pasta, you'd need something a little stronger: I like to use type 0 flour, which you can get at Italian markets; high-quality all-purpose flour from King Arthur, which has an 11.7 percent protein content, will work, too.

- **2 pounds Yukon gold potatoes, scrubbed**

- **Sea salt**

- **Pinch of freshly grated nutmeg** (optional)

- **At least ½ cup type 0 flour** (see headnote) **or high-quality all-purpose flour, for rolling and dusting**

- **1 large egg yolk**

- **Parmigiano-Reggiano, for serving**

1. Bake the potatoes at 350°F until they're fork tender (see headnote). If you're boiling the potatoes, boil until tender, but not falling apart.

2. Halve the potatoes and scoop out the flesh if they're baked, or peel them if they're boiled. Then mash them using a potato ricer or food mill. Season the potatoes with salt and the grated nutmeg, if using.

3. Flour your work surface, then pile ¼ cup of the flour on top. Next to it, pile the warm potatoes in a mound (you want to work with them right away; if they cool down, they'll become gluey and sticky). Create a well in the middle of the potatoes. Working from the pile of flour, sprinkle a thin layer in the well, then carefully place the yolk on top. Dip back into the pile of flour and sprinkle enough on top of the yolk to cover it. Here comes the fun part: Using your fingers, scoop a bit of potato into the well, break the yolk, and add more potatoes. Work in a little more flour from the pile. Continue mixing the potatoes and yolk together, incorporating the flour a little bit at a time, using just enough to keep the dough from breaking apart. Don't be afraid of the stickiness of the dough! It needs to come together just enough to hold, which will take only a few minutes; resist the temptation to overwork it. When you're done, it should be soft and pillowy.

4. Flour a large plate or a baking sheet and place it next to your work surface, then flour your work surface again. Tear off a piece of the dough and roll it into a long log a little thicker than your thumb. Using a knife, cut the log crosswise into dime-sized pieces. (How big or small you want to make the pieces is up to you; just make sure they're roughly the same size so they'll cook in the same amount of time.) You can leave the pieces as is, or roll them down a gnocchi board to create ridges. Place the pieces on the floured plate or baking sheet. Repeat with the rest of the dough.

5. You can freeze the gnocchi at this point: Place the plate or baking sheet directly into your freezer. Once the individual pieces are frozen, transfer them to a resealable bag and store in the freezer for the next time you need a quick, easy meal. They'll be good for up to 3 months.

6. To cook the gnocchi, boil a large pot of generously salted water (it should taste like seawater). Shake as much of the flour off the gnocchi as you can and drop the pieces into the boiling water in batches so you don't crowd the pot. Boil the gnocchi for just a few minutes, until they float, then pull them out with a strainer. Repeat with the remaining gnocchi. (Frozen gnocchi can be cooked straight from the freezer; they'll take a minute or two longer.)

7. Divide the boiled gnocchi among bowls and add a grating of Parmesan on top.

# Temperature and Flavor

**A** **FEW YEARS AGO,** researchers isolated a taste receptor on the tongue that not only picks up umami (as well as bitter and sweet flavors) but also is sensitive to the temperature of a food: The warmer the food, the stronger those specific flavors seem to be. That said, a dish or a drink that's too hot will actually mask flavor rather than enhance it.

At the other extreme, cold can affect flavor, too. Take the tomato: It has one of the highest levels of glutamates of all produce. But surely we've all had the experience of pulling a tomato from the fridge only to be sorely disappointed by how utterly flavorless it is. One culprit for that blandness is the chill of the fridge. University of Florida researchers found out not too long ago that in cold environments, the genes that control the tomato's flavor turn off. Supermarket tomatoes are often stored at cold temperatures before they hit the shelves, meaning there's a good chance that the tomatoes from the market have already lost a ton of flavor before you've even brought them home. There's no rehabilitating them from that. If you want tomatoes at their peak umami level, try to buy them fresh from the farmers' market and don't refrigerate them. If tomatoes aren't in season, use high-quality canned tomatoes instead.

Wine and beer also have flavor compounds that are either suppressed or released depending on temperature. Rosés and white wines often have a fruity sweetness that's accentuated by the cold; heavy-bodied red wines and stouts, on the other hand, benefit from a warmer temperature to bring out their aromatics. Depending on what flavors you want to bring out and taste, either chill or warm up the bottle before pouring. It's a simple thing to do but will make a huge difference in what you taste.

# CRAB-EGG CLOUDS

**T**HIS IS A FUN LUNCH FOR THE KIDS OR for you, especially those times when you're too exhausted to do much more than whip up some eggs. The eggs are whisked while they're slowly cooked to a silky consistency, like little crab-transporting clouds. The crab and its umami flavor complete the dish.

- 4 ounces backfin blue crabmeat
- 1 tablespoon unsalted butter
- Pinch of herbes de Provence
- 3 large eggs, at room temperature and lightly beaten
- 1 tablespoon crème fraîche
- 1 tablespoon chopped fresh chives
- Sea salt and freshly ground white pepper
- Freshly grated Parmigiano-Reggiano

1. In a small skillet over low heat, cook the crabmeat with the butter. Add the herbes de Provence, stir, and pour in the eggs and crème fraîche. Beat the crab and egg using a whisk until the eggs are slightly curdy, about 3 minutes. Turn off the heat.

2. To serve, carefully slide the eggs out onto a plate. Sprinkle the chopped chives and some salt and pepper on top, and finish with the freshly grated Parmesan. Serve immediately.

# PRAWNS MOJO DE AJO

**M**OJO DE AJO IS AN AWESOME ALL-PURPOSE GARLIC sauce that's a staple in Latin American cooking. Everyone has their own version of mojo de ajo that involves varying amounts of garlic, lime juice, oil, and salt; in mine I roast the garlic first to really deepen its flavor. From there I toss it with prawns. I prefer to use spot prawns because they are bigger and meatier and won't overcook as easily as shrimp. If you can't find spot prawns, ask your fishmonger to pick out large head-on prawns, or sub in high-quality wild-caught shrimp from a responsible source. Store any leftover sauce in the fridge. It is tasty on anything savory.

### MOJO DE AJO

- ◆ **2 heads garlic, unpeeled**
- ◆ **Extra-virgin olive oil**
- ◆ **Splash of dry white wine—use whatever white wine you're drinking**
- ◆ **Splash of white wine vinegar**
- ◆ **1 teaspoon fresh lime juice**
- ◆ **Sea salt and freshly ground black pepper**
- ◆ **1 tablespoon unsalted butter**

### PRAWNS

- ◆ **1 pound spot prawns or large head-on prawns** (see headnote)
- ◆ **2 tablespoons olive oil**
- ◆ **2 tablespoons unsalted butter**
- ◆ **4 slices rustic bread**

*continued*

1. **MAKE THE MOJO DE AJO:** Preheat the oven to 350°F, with a rack in the top.

2. Cut just enough off the top of the garlic heads to expose the cloves, and drizzle a good amount of olive oil directly on top of the cloves, enough to really coat the garlic generously. Wrap both heads, together or separately, in aluminum foil and place on the rack. Bake until the garlic is soft, deeply golden, and your kitchen (if not your whole house) is thick with the aroma of garlic, about an hour. The cloves should be a deep tan, but not black.

3. Once the garlic has cooled enough for you to handle, pop the cloves out of their paper skins into a food processor (or mortar), and puree the garlic with the splashes of white wine and white wine vinegar, the lime juice, a splash of extra-virgin olive oil, some salt and pepper, and the butter. It should form a thickened sauce. Set aside to let the flavors meld.

4. **MAKE THE PRAWNS:** Peel the prawns, leaving the head and tail intact (see Flavor Tip). Place the olive oil and butter in a large skillet over medium heat, then sauté the prawns until they're just opaque, a few minutes. Remove the prawns to a plate, and add the bread slices to the skillet. Toast each side for 2 minutes (you can also grill the bread if you'd prefer).

5. To serve, put a slice or two of toast on some plates. Place a few prawns on each slice, then spoon a generous helping of mojo de ajo on top. Leave a bowl of mojo de ajo on the table for anyone who might want more. Dive in.

**FLAVOR TIP**

Shrimp and prawn heads have a ton of umami, so give one a try if you're not otherwise accustomed to eating them. They are delicious.

# SMOKED DUCK BREASTS

SERVES 4

**T**HESE DUCK BREASTS ARE SMOKED FOR A FEW HOURS, THEN finished in a cast-iron pan or on the grill. Serve this with Umami'd Fregola Sarda (page 214) or with a steamed Japanese purple yam fork-mashed with butter.

- 4 duck breasts, about 6 ounces each
- Olive oil
- 2 tablespoons truffle honey or wildflower honey
- Aged balsamic vinegar

1. Smoke the breasts in a smoker at 250°F, using mild woods like apple, cherry, or pecan, for 2 hours. The duck will be nearly, but not completely, done at this point, but the skins should be a nice golden brown. If you don't have a smoker, you can also pan-smoke by lining a Dutch oven or a roasting pan with foil. Place the chips on top of the foil and a rack on top of the chips. Heat on the stove over medium heat. When you see wisps of smoke coming from the chips, place the duck breasts on the rack and cover.

2. Remove the breasts from the smoker. Place a large cast-iron skillet over high heat on your stove and add a glug of olive oil. Finish cooking the duck breasts by searing them skin side down in the skillet for 6 minutes, until the skin is nice and crispy. Sear in batches if your pan isn't big enough to work with them all at the same time. Alternatively, if you already have the grill going, you can sear the duck directly on the grill.

3. When you have a nice sear on the breasts, flip them over and, using a spoon, glaze the skin with the honey. Right before digging in, drizzle the balsamic vinegar over the duck.

# DUCK BREASTS with PORT GLAZE

SERVES 4

**P**ORT WINE, HONEY, A FEW SELECT SPICES, AND A secret ingredient—a generous helping of Umami Master Sauce—combine to make a delicious glaze for duck breasts. The crucial step is to score the skin of the duck breasts. If you don't, the fatty duck will stay fatty, and the skin won't get nice and crisp. Serve the duck breasts with a side of vegetables, rice, or potatoes.

- **4 duck breasts, 7 to 8 ounces each**
- ½ cup honey
- ½ cup good port
- **¼ cup Umami Master Sauce** (page 34)
- ½ cinnamon stick
- 3 cloves
- 3 allspice berries
- 1 star anise
- ½ teaspoon black peppercorns
- Sea salt and freshly ground black pepper

1. Preheat the oven to 425°F.

2. If your butcher hasn't already done it for you, carefully remove any excess overhanging skin and fat from around each duck breast and discard.

3. Next, score the breasts. If you haven't ever done this before, it's easy: There is a thick layer of fat between the skin and the meat of the duck; scoring the skin will allow that fat to render as the meat cooks (see Flavor Tip) and give you a beautifully crisp skin. To score it, use a sharp knife or a razor to make shallow diagonal slashes in the skin ¼ inch to ½ inch apart. Be careful to not cut *through* the skin and into the fat and meat, otherwise you'll lose the precious juices in the duck and it'll dry out faster when it cooks. Then rotate the breast and slash diagonally again so you end up with a crisscrossing pattern on the skin. Repeat for the other duck breasts, then set them aside while you prepare the sauce.

4. In a small saucepan over medium-low heat, simmer the honey and port until reduced by about half, skimming off any impurities. When the sauce has reduced, mix in the master sauce, cinnamon stick, cloves, allspice, star anise, and peppercorns. Kill the heat and set aside to cool. When it's at room temp, strain the sauce.

5. Place a large cast-iron skillet or other ovenproof skillet over medium heat. Season all sides of the duck breasts with a good pinch of salt and pepper. Wait a minute or two for the skillet to get good and hot, then place the duck breasts skin side down in the pan, giving them enough room so the skins sear nicely (use two pans if all four breasts don't fit in one pan). When the duck breasts hit the pan, they should immediately sizzle and pop as the fat renders. (Notice we didn't add any oil to the pan—this rendering fat is all the grease you need.)

6. When the skins are crispy and golden brown, 5 to 7 minutes, flip the breasts over and sear the other sides for just 1 minute. (If a breast sticks a little when you first try to move it, let it cook a little longer; the duck will release when it's ready.) Take the breasts out of the pan and brush on the honey-port sauce. Place them all in one pan and into the oven. I like my duck breasts medium-rare, so I bake them for 6 to 7 minutes, but go a minute or two longer if you prefer them cooked through more.

7. Let the duck breasts rest for at least 3 minutes before slicing and serving.

FLAVOR TIP

After searing the duck breasts and pulling them out of the pan to glaze, don't throw away any of the fat you've rendered. Duck fat is versatile, which is why I keep it in my fridge at all times. Use it to fry your eggs, or in the Salmon in Tomato-Truffle Butter (page 58).

# CHICKEN CONFIT
## WITH DIRTY FARRO

SERVES 4

**Y**ES, THE INGREDIENT LIST FOR THIS RECIPE IS LONG, BUT ONCE you get everything prepped out, you don't have a lot more to do, and nothing is difficult in terms of technique—the bulk of the cooking is passive. For the confit, the chicken cooks low and slow in the duck fat, and the grains cook in the umamified broth. Don't leave out the livers—it wouldn't be dirty farro without them. Once you mix them in with the umamified grains, you won't even know they're there.

Farro has a chewiness and nuttiness that goes well with the multiple umami ingredients in the broth. If you don't have farro on hand, you can also use rice (try the Umami'd Rice, page 212). Whether you use farro or rice, this is a deliciously Southern-ish dish perfect to make for a meal with friends. Serve with Fried Sweet Onion Strings (page 203) or a side of roasted vegetables.

### CHICKEN

- 21 ounces (about 2½ cups) duck fat
- 1 pound skinless, boneless chicken thighs, trimmed (see Flavor Tip)

### FARRO

- 1½ cups chicken stock, plus more if needed for the pork
- 3 dried porcini mushrooms
- 3 dried morel mushrooms, rinsed in cold water to remove any grit or dirt
- Dash of fish sauce
- Dash of Worcestershire sauce

- 1 (4-by-4-inch) piece kombu
- 1 cup farro, rinsed
- Sea salt and freshly ground black pepper
- 4 ounces chicken livers
- 4 ounces ground pork shoulder (ideally, freshly ground at home using your food processor as you would grind your own beef to make burgers [see page 102], but you can also use pre-ground pork)
- 2 tablespoons olive oil
- Pinch of togarashi
- ½ medium onion, finely diced
- 2 garlic cloves, minced
- ½ jalapeño, stemmed, seeded, and chopped
- 1 teaspoon dried oregano
- 1 tablespoon chopped scallion, green and white parts
- 1 tablespoon fresh flat-leaf parsley
- Fried Sweet Onion Strings (optional; page 203), for serving

1. **CONFIT THE CHICKEN:** Put the duck fat in a large pot over low heat (if the duck fat is frozen, you'll need to melt it in the pot first). Submerge the thighs in the fat. Cook until the juices in the chicken run clear and the thighs are cooked through. This will take anywhere between 20 and 40 minutes, depending on how low you go with the flame. There's no need to rush this; take as long as you need.

2. **MAKE THE FARRO:** Pour the 1½ cups of chicken stock into a medium saucepan over high heat and add the mushrooms, fish sauce, and Worcestershire sauce. Bring to a boil, then add the kombu. Boil for 2 minutes, stirring, then fish out the kombu and toss it out.

3. While the broth is still at a boil, add the farro, then drop the heat down to medium and let it simmer. Season with salt and pepper. Depending on how al dente you like your farro, it'll take 25 to 35 minutes to cook. This can be done up to a day in advance of mealtime. (If you're making rice instead, follow the method for Umami'd Rice on page 212, or the directions on the rice package.)

4. Meanwhile, place the chicken livers and pork in a blender or food processor and puree until well combined and mostly smooth. Set the mixture aside in the fridge.

5. Taste the farro. When it's almost at the level of bite you like, place a large skillet over medium heat and add the olive oil. Take the liver and pork mixture out of the fridge and, when the oil is nice and hot, add it to the pan. Let the mix sizzle for a few seconds to brown, then stir to break up the meat and brown on all sides. Season with the togarashi and a pinch of salt and pepper.

*continued*

6. Once the puree is browned, throw in the onion, garlic, jalapeño, and oregano. Stir to combine.

7. Scoop out ¼ cup of the stock from the farro pot (or use additional stock from the container, if needed) and pour it into the liver and pork mix to deglaze the pan. Once the liquid has mostly evaporated, add in the farro, including any of its liquid. Throw in the scallion and parsley. Stir, stir, stir. Turn off the heat.

8. Pull the chicken thighs out of the fat and place on top of the farro. (Strain the fat and stash it in the fridge, covered—you can reuse it.) If you made them, heap the Fried Sweet Onion Strings on top, too. Serve right from the skillet. As with a good casserole, the flavors will only meld as time passes. In fact, this is far better after it sits for a few hours.

9. This will keep, covered, in the fridge for up to 2 days. To reheat, place it in an ovenproof dish and warm it up in a 250°F oven for 15 minutes.

## FLAVOR TIP

Most chefs, me included, use dark meat in chicken dishes because you can cook it off the bone without worrying about it drying out. But if you prefer white meat, you can use it here, though don't skin or debone it before cooking. Instead, keep the skin on and the bone in so the meat retains its moisture.

# PUERTO RICAN MOFONGO

**SERVES 2**

**M**OFONGO IS A CLASSIC PUERTO RICAN DISH WITH PLANTAINS front and center, literally: The plantains are placed in the middle of the plate. I top the mofongo with chicken and a pan sauce. The dish gets much of its flavor from the pan sauce, which you'll make after searing the chicken and a few vegetables and deglazing the pan with stock. If you don't have stock, use a premade demi-glace—I like the ones from Savory Choice—and dilute it in water. It all comes together in minutes.

Note: Many major supermarkets carry plantains nowadays, but if you're out of luck there, try picking up a bunch at your local Mexican, Central American, or Asian market.

- ◆ **2 green plantains**
- ◆ **3 tablespoons olive oil**
- ◆ **2 garlic cloves, minced**
- ◆ **2 skinless, boneless chicken breasts or 4 skinless, boneless thighs, or a combination**
- ◆ **2 medium tomatoes, chopped**
- ◆ **1 green bell pepper, cored, seeded, and chopped**
- ◆ **1 medium onion, chopped**
- ◆ **2 tablespoons tomato paste**
- ◆ **1 cup chicken stock, or ½ cup chicken demi-glace (such as Savory Choice Chicken Demi-Glace) diluted in ½ cup water, or a combination**
- ◆ **2 teaspoons unsalted butter**
- ◆ **Sea salt and freshly ground black pepper**
- ◆ **½ cup fresh cilantro leaves, chopped**

1. Peel and slice the plantains into ¼-inch coins. Place a tablespoon of olive oil in a large skillet over medium heat and cook the sliced plantains with half of the minced garlic until the plantains are soft, about 10 minutes. Transfer the plantains and garlic to a food processor and pulse a few times, or enough to incorporate the ingredients while still keeping the plantains chunky. For a fancy presentation, put the plantains into a ring mold on a plate and then remove the ring to unmold. Or, if that is too fussy for you, forget the mold and just pile the plantains in a neat mound on the plate.

2. In the same skillet that you just used to cook the plantains, up the heat to high and add another tablespoon of olive oil. Wait a minute or so to let the pan get hot, then sear the chicken on both sides until it's almost cooked through, 7 to 8 minutes per side if using breasts, or 5 to 7 minutes per side if using thighs. Transfer the chicken to a cutting board and chop it into cubes.

3. Back in the same pan, over medium heat, add a tablespoon of oil and sauté the tomatoes, bell pepper, onion, the remaining garlic, and the tomato paste until the vegetables are soft, about 4 minutes. Pour the chicken stock into the pan to deglaze, using a spoon to scrape the delicious browned bits off the bottom of the pan. Add the butter and season with salt and pepper. Reduce until slightly thickened, about 2 minutes.

4. Let the vegetable mix cool slightly, then transfer to the food processor and process until liquefied. Strain the mixture through a fine-mesh sieve or a coffee filter back into the pan, add the cubed chicken, and cook for just a few minutes, or until the chicken is cooked all the way through. Pour the chicken and its sauce over the plantains and top with the chopped cilantro. Serve.

# STEAKS

## WITH FANCY MAKE-AHEAD RESTAURANT SAUCE

**A** GREAT STEAK IS NOT HARD TO MAKE. AS WITH A BURGER PATTY, the success of steak rests on the method: You need a hot pan to trigger the Maillard reaction and bring out all those nice caramelized flavors. The brown bits left after searing form the base for the steak sauce. Most recipes call for you to make the sauce in the pan after you've seared the steaks, but if you're as impatient to eat as I am, make the sauce ahead of time instead and use it to deglaze the pan. The steaks rest just as long as they need to, and you get to eat faster.

These steaks are great over any kind of potato or vegetable preparation, like Fried Sweet Onion Strings (page 203) or Quick-Cooked Japanese-Style Collards (page 198).

- **2 steaks (6 to 8 ounces each), preferably filets mignons, trimmed and pounded ½ inch thick; or New York strip loins or boneless rib-eye steaks with the fat trimmed**
- Sea salt and freshly ground black pepper
- 1 tablespoon grapeseed oil
- **1 recipe Fancy Make-Ahead Restaurant Sauce** (opposite)
- 1 tablespoon chopped fresh chives

1. Season the steaks generously with salt and pepper. Heat the oil in a large cast-iron skillet over high heat. Add the steaks and sear all sides, working with one steak at a time if necessary to avoid crowding the pan. When seared dark (but not past medium-rare), about 8 minutes total, remove the steaks to a cutting board or plate.

2. Add the sauce to the pan to deglaze it, stirring to scrape up the browned bits on the bottom. Keep stirring for another minute or two, until the sauce is slightly reduced and thickened.

3. Add the steaks back to the pan and spoon the sauce over them. Serve garnished with the chives.

# FANCY MAKE-AHEAD RESTAURANT SAUCE

## MAKES ENOUGH FOR 2 STEAKS

THIS SAUCE IS BASED ON STEAK DIANE, THAT OLD-SCHOOL dish that was the toast of every fancy restaurant in the 1970s. It's usually made with shallot, mustard, cream, and brandy or cognac, plus a dash of Worcestershire, but I add anchovies and aged cheese to heighten the umami factor. You can also throw this sauce on chicken, pork, fresh porcinis, or a really meaty white fish.

- 1½ cups water
- **5 dried porcini mushrooms**
- 1 shallot, finely chopped
- 1 tablespoon unsalted butter
- Sea salt and freshly ground black pepper
- Splash of brandy
- **2 tablespoons beef demi-glace or stock**
- **3 ounces Roquefort or Gorgonzola, crumbled**
- **2 anchovy fillets**
- 1 tablespoon Dijon mustard
- ½ cup heavy cream or crème fraîche

1. In a small saucepan over low heat, warm 1 cup of the water. Turn off the heat and add the dried porcinis. Soak the mushrooms until they're completely rehydrated, 20 to 30 minutes. Strain the water through a fine-mesh sieve or coffee filter; discard any grit or dirt and set the water aside with the mushrooms.

2. Add the shallot to a small skillet with the butter over medium heat and cook until the shallot is translucent. Add a small pinch of salt and pepper. Carefully add the brandy and, using a lighter or a long match set right above the edge of the pan, ignite, making sure to avert your face.

3. As soon as the flames die down, add the mushrooms and their liquid, the demi-glace or stock, and the remaining ½ cup of water to the pan. Bring to a boil over medium heat. Add the cheese, anchovies, mustard, and cream, whisking for 30 seconds, then take the pan off the heat. Carefully pour everything into a blender and puree into a sauce.

4. You can make this up to a day ahead; store leftovers in a covered container in the fridge and use within a week.

# CHAMPIONSHIP CHILI

MAKES 2 QUARTS CHILI, WHICH WILL SERVE A PARTY OF 6 TO 8

**M**OST PEOPLE THINK OF CHILI AS A QUICK MEAL, SOMETHING you make with beans. Which is a shame, because when you take the time to make it right, chili is full of flavors and textures, able to stand on its own, with or without beans.

Fundamentally, chili is a braise. A great all-American, umamified braise. I use an 80/20 ratio of chuck to chorizo: cubed chuck and ground chuck for texture and chorizo for fat and to hit a bit of a spice note. After browning, the meat goes right into the liquids to be braised for 4 or so hours. Anything that's overcooked will soften, and anything that's not cooked through will definitely finish during the long braising process. Then it sits in the fridge overnight, developing layers of flavor. This is a very, very forgiving recipe, and you can always fix the seasoning as you go. If you don't have a few things handy in your pantry, use what you do have and adjust to taste along the way.

I've won chili cook-offs with this recipe. You will, too.

Eat the chili by itself or serve it over spaghetti with some cheddar cheese grated on top. Eat it with rice. Ladle it over a hot dog or eat it in a burger. Use it as a dip for tortilla chips. The possibilities are endless.

- 2 tablespoons olive oil
- 1 large or 2 medium onions, diced
- 2 large garlic cloves, minced
- Canola oil
- 1 pound cubed beef, preferably chuck or brisket
- 1 (12-ounce) bottle lager beer, or another beer that's not too hoppy
- 1 pound ground beef, preferably chuck or brisket
- 8 ounces Mexican chorizo
- 1 cup beef stock, plus more if needed
- 1 cup chicken stock
- 2 teaspoons Umami Master Sauce (page 34)
- 1 teaspoon Worcestershire sauce
- ½ teaspoon fish sauce
- ½ teaspoon hot sauce
- 2 ounces dried porcini mushrooms, soaked in warm water for 20 to 30 minutes to rehydrate, then strained to remove grit and dirt
- 1 (28-ounce) can whole peeled tomatoes, preferably from Italy or California
- 2 teaspoons tomato paste
- 2 bay leaves
- 1 cinnamon stick, preferably Mexican
- ½ cup Chili Spice Blend (page 173), plus more to taste
- 1 tablespoon sorghum, honey, or molasses
- 2 ounces dark chocolate, grated

OPTIONAL GARNISHES

- Fresh cilantro
- Smoked sea salt
- Pimentón (smoked paprika)
- Hot sauce

1. Place the olive oil in a large stockpot or a Dutch oven over medium-low heat, then throw in the onion and garlic. Let them cook down until very soft (but not browned), about 10 minutes, while you get started on the meat.

2. In another pan—the biggest skillet you can fit on your burners—over high heat, add a tablespoon of canola oil and just enough of the cubed beef to cover the skillet in one layer. Don't crowd the pan, or else the meat will steam instead of brown (see Flavor Tip). Brown the beef in batches if it doesn't all fit.

3. Once the beef is nicely browned on all sides, about 5 minutes, carefully add it to the stockpot with the onion and garlic. Now, deglaze: Add some of the beer (leave some for later) to your browning pan and use a spoon or spatula to scrape up the browned bits on the bottom of the pan (see Flavor Tip).

4. After deglazing, add the liquid and the scraped-up bits to the stockpot.

5. If working in batches, repeat this process of browning and deglazing with the rest of the cubed beef (don't forget to add a tablespoon of canola oil between batches). When you're done with the cubed beef, move on to the ground beef and chorizo. Add both meats to the pan and stir the two together as you brown them.

6. As the ground beef and chorizo brown, turn to the stockpot. Raise the heat to medium and keep things at a simmer as you add the beef and chicken stocks, Umami Master Sauce, Worcestershire sauce, fish sauce, hot sauce, and the rehydrated mushrooms and their liquid. When you're done deglazing the meat with the beer, pour the rest of the bottle into this stockpot, too.

*continued*

7. Next, add the tomatoes and their liquid, tomato paste, bay leaves, cinnamon stick, and about three quarters of the Chili Spice Blend. Note that we're not adding salt; there's already plenty in the other ingredients.

8. Mix in the sorghum, honey, or molasses (which will give the chili a bit of sweetness and tame some of the spices) and the chocolate. Taste and adjust the seasonings if you think the chili needs it.

9. After the beef and chorizo have browned, add them to the pot.

10. Once all the ground beef and chorizo are in the main stockpot, bring the whole thing to a boil, then bring it down to a very low simmer. An occasional bubble is perfect.

11. That's it. Let this go for about 4 hours, stirring occasionally. Or, if you need room on the stove, stick the pot in the oven at 250°F instead for 4 hours. Check on the chili every once in a while and stir. If it's a little dry, add a little extra beef stock. Taste it again. If the chili needs some extra spice, or you realize you forgot an ingredient, throw it in.

12. After 4 hours, the chili should have a nice, thick, velvety consistency and a rusty red color. The meat should be so tender that it'll fall apart with a nudge of a fork. If there's still a lot of liquid in the pot, raise the heat to high and boil it off. Taste again. If you think it needs a little more spice or seasoning, add a few shakes of the chili blend. When everything tastes right, stick it in the fridge, covered, and let it sit overnight.

13. When you're ready to serve, taste and adjust the seasonings again. If the chili thickened too much, no biggie. Add some water until it is the desired consistency. Remove the bay leaves and cinnamon stick. For garnish, throw in a little fresh cilantro, which will brighten things up, and finish with a bit of smoked salt or pimentón, or both.

14. Have hot sauce out on the table.

15. Leftovers can be placed in an airtight container and refrigerated for up to 3 days, or frozen for up to 2 months.

## FLAVOR TIPS

Never rush the browning process. Browning, in fact, is the most important step in braising; it'll trigger the Maillard reaction and will give the meat a ton of flavor. If the meat starts to turn gray, don't pull it out—let it continue to cook until it really, truly browns.

Always deglaze the pan at the end of any browning process. All the bits at the bottom of the pan—called the *fond* in French—are full of flavor.

# CHILI SPICE BLEND

**MAKES AS MUCH AS YOU WANT TO MAKE**

THIS DRY RUB IS GREAT TO THROW INTO THE CHILI; it's also great as an all-purpose dry rub for any meat or poultry. I like dark chili powder for this—it's smokier than regular chili powder because it's been roasted longer—but regular chili powder is fine, too.

**TO MAKE THE BLEND, YOU'LL NEED EQUAL PORTIONS OF:**

- Ground dried pasilla chile
- Ground dried ancho chile
- Ground dried chipotle chile
- Garlic powder
- Ground cumin
- Pimentón (smoked paprika)
- Freshly ground black pepper
- **Ground dried porcini mushrooms**
- Dark-roast chili powder (see headnote)

1. Mix the spices together in a small bowl. Use as needed as a dry rub.

2. Store the spice blend in your pantry, covered, for up to 6 months.

# SWEET AND SAVORY BRISKET

SERVES 8

**E**VERY COOK WORTH THEIR SALT BRAISES. TIME INFUSES a rich savoriness with ineffable depth. While I use plenty of umami ingredients to elevate this brisket—soy sauce, fish sauce, dried mushrooms—it's really the clock that unlocks the flavor by allowing the ingredients to meld and integrate. Indeed, long cooking is often the key to greatness: Umami + Time = Flavor. That's my brisket.

You can use the leftovers to make a Faster Bolognese Sauce (page 128) or as the meat layer in the Umami-Layered Tart (page 72).

- 3 tablespoons olive oil, plus more if needed
- 1½ pounds onions (about 2 large onions), sliced into half-moons
- Sea salt and freshly ground black pepper
- ¼ cup aged balsamic vinegar, plus more for the braise
- 4½ pounds beef brisket (the fattier the better—Wagyu is the best because it has more fat)
- 16 garlic cloves, 4 minced, 12 peeled and left whole
- 3 cups chicken stock

- 2 tablespoons soy sauce
- 2 tablespoons fish sauce
- 2 tablespoons Umami Ketchup (page 35)
- 8 dried porcini mushrooms, rinsed in cold water to remove dirt and grit
- 8 dried morel mushrooms, rinsed in cold water to remove dirt and grit
- Dash of hot sauce
- 2 tablespoons Vadouvan (optional; page 42)

1. Preheat the oven to 325°F.

2. Heat 1 tablespoon of the olive oil in a deep sauté pan or cast-iron skillet over medium heat. Add the onions and cook on medium-low to medium heat, stirring frequently, for about 1 hour, or until they have caramelized (see page 41). Season with salt and pepper and deglaze with ¼ cup of the balsamic. Keep the bottle of balsamic out; you'll need a splash of it right before the brisket goes into the oven.

3. Meanwhile, pat the brisket dry. Season it generously with salt and pepper, then sprinkle the minced garlic over the meat.

4. Place 2 tablespoons of the olive oil in a skillet or Dutch oven large enough to fit the brisket over medium-high heat and turn on your vent or fan if you have one: It's going to get smoky. Sear the brisket on all sides until a golden-brown crust forms, adding more olive oil as necessary. Remove and place in a roasting pan, fatty side up.

5. Pile the onions on top of and around the meat.

6. On the stovetop, place the chicken stock in a small saucepan and add in the soy sauce, fish sauce, Umami Ketchup, dried porcinis, dried morels, hot sauce, Vadouvan (if using), and a splash of the balsamic. Stir and bring the mixture to almost a boil. Remove from the heat and pour over the brisket. Scatter the 12 remaining garlic cloves around the meat and cover tightly with foil. Place in the oven and braise for 4 to 5 hours, until very tender.

7. Remove the brisket from the oven and slice to serve, with some of the sauce spooned over it.

---

NOTE

This brisket is even better the next day: Let the meat cool completely but don't slice it, then refrigerate it overnight. When you're ready to serve, preheat the oven to 300°F. Meanwhile, remove the brisket from the pan and scrape away and discard the layer of fat that has formed around the meat. Slice the brisket and return it to the pan. Cover with a lid or two layers of foil and warm in the oven for about 1 hour.

# OSSO BUCO

**SSO BUCO IS A CLASSIC,** *classic* Italian braise, with veal shanks that cook in a broth of wine and tomatoes. I reinforce the glutamate-rich veal and tomatoes with a few additional umami ingredients like mushrooms and fish sauce. Make this tonight, then use any leftovers to make Veal Marsala Pasta (page 144) tomorrow night (or double this recipe and stash half of it for the pasta). Osso buco is even better as leftovers, after the braise has had time to sit and meld for a day.

Serve the veal on top of a potato puree, rice, or other starch of your choice.

**SERVES 4**

- 1 cup water
- ½ cup dried morel mushrooms
- 1½ pounds veal shanks
- Sea salt and freshly ground black pepper
- 2 tablespoons extra-virgin olive oil
- 1 teaspoon veal demi-glace, veal stock, beef demi-glace, or beef stock
- 3 cups chicken stock
- 2 tablespoons tomato paste

- 1 sprig thyme
- Splash of fish sauce
- 1 tablespoon Umami Master Dust (page 32)
- 1 tablespoon Umami Master Sauce (page 34)
- 1 fresh pequín pepper or other small fresh red chile, coarsely chopped
- 2 small onions, chopped
- Splash of dry sherry

1. In a small saucepan over low heat, warm the water. Turn off the heat and add the dried morels. Soak the mushrooms until they're completely rehydrated, 20 to 30 minutes. Strain the water through a fine-mesh sieve or coffee filter; discard any grit or dirt and set the water aside with the mushrooms.

2. Sear the meat: Season the veal shanks with salt and pepper. Place the olive oil in a large skillet over high heat. When the pan starts to smoke, carefully add the veal and sear on all sides until deeply caramelized, about 4 minutes total. Work in batches if necessary.

3. Meanwhile, prepare your braising liquid. In a large stockpot or Dutch oven over medium heat, add the veal or beef demi-glace or stock, chicken stock, tomato paste, sprigs of rosemary and thyme, the morels and their liquid, fish sauce, Umami Master Dust, Umami Master Sauce, the red chile, and onions. Stir to combine.

4. Add the seared veal to the pot. Deglaze the veal pan with the splash of sherry, scraping up the caramelized bits in the pan. Pour it all into the pot.

5. Bring the contents of the pot to a boil, then reduce the heat to a simmer. Braise the veal for 3 hours, uncovered, stirring occasionally, until the liquid has reduced substantially and the veal is super tender.

6. Discard the herb sprigs. Serve.

# Fat and Flavor

**O**IL, BUTTER, AND DUCK fat are the main fats I use in my cooking, and without them, a lot of my dishes wouldn't be as interesting. That's because fats carry and distribute flavor. Crush some garlic and sauté it in some oil and you'll notice that the oil is now flavored with it. Throw in some spinach on top of that and the greens, too, will pick up a nice garlicky flavor. Fat also coats your mouth, so whatever flavors are trapped in the fat will linger on your palate, even after you've swallowed your bite.

The fat in meat also holds flavor, which is why a highly marbled steak is preferable to a cut that's lean: When you cook steak, the fat melts and unleashes all the stored flavors into the meat itself. The melting fat, of course, also tenderizes the meat as it cooks, so it stays juicy. The specific flavor stored in the fat depends in part on what the animal was fed. A grass-fed lamb, for example, will taste distinctly different from one that was fed a diet of grains.

Fat plays such a prominent role in how we taste and perceive food that it's been the subject of many studies on how we process its taste. Recently scientists isolated receptors in our tongue that can pick up fatty acids, which has led some to argue that fat itself should be considered our sixth taste, after sweet, salty, sour, bitter, and, of course, umami.

# MARMITE SWEET-AND-SOUR PORK

**SERVES 4**

## PORK

- 1 large egg white
- Freshly ground black pepper
- 1 tablespoon Umami Master Sauce (page 34)
- 1 pound pork tenderloin, cut into 1-inch cubes
- 2 cups vegetable oil
- 1 cup cornstarch

## SAUCE

- 2 tablespoons Marmite (see headnote)
- 1 tablespoon Umami Master Sauce (page 34)
- 2½ tablespoons honey
- ½ cup water
- 2½ tablespoons Umami Ketchup (page 35)

**Y**EAST EXTRACTS ARE HUGE sources of umami, and Marmite (see page 25) is probably the most famous yeast extract product of them all. It's popular in the United Kingdom and Australia, where it's often eaten on toast, but most Americans don't like it very much straight out of the jar. Here, in this piquant sweet-and-sour sauce, the intensity of the Marmite is balanced by the sweetness from the honey and ketchup. Serve with Umami'd Rice (page 212) or regular white rice.

1. MAKE THE PORK: In a large bowl, whisk together the egg white, a pinch of pepper, and the master sauce. Add the pork to the bowl, toss it all together, and marinate, refrigerated, for 1 hour.

2. Place the vegetable oil in a large saucepan over medium heat.

3. Meanwhile, place the cornstarch in a large resealable bag. Throw in the pork and dredge to coat the pieces. Grab some paper towels and place them on a baking sheet next to the saucepan.

4. When the oil is hot, add the pork pieces in a single layer to the pan and sear on all sides. You want each piece of pork to have enough elbow room to sear properly or they will steam instead, so if the pieces don't have about an inch of space between them, work in batches. It should take about 2 to 3 minutes per batch. Drain the pork on the paper towels.

5. **MAKE THE SAUCE:** Heat a wok or large skillet and add the Marmite, master sauce, and honey. Stir to combine, then add the water. Simmer the sauce for a few minutes to reduce and thicken it a bit, then whisk in the ketchup. Adjust the seasonings to taste. Reduce the sauce for a few minutes more, until it's thick and glaze-like.

6. Add the pork and turn the pieces to coat and warm up. Serve.

---

**FLAVOR TIP**

Marmite has what is sometimes called palate persistence: Its flavor lingers on your palate even after you've taken a bite. Notably, that's exactly what a lot of the chemical flavor "enhancers" on the market actually do. They don't create any new flavors at all; instead they just make the flavors last. This sauce proves you can achieve the same thing with the judicious use of umami ingredients.

# ROQUEFORT AND MUSHROOM FONDUE

**SERVES 4**

**I FIRST STARTED MAKING THIS FONDUE FOR PARTIES MORE THAN A** decade ago. I wanted something easy and tasty that I could make in advance, then keep warm and serve as my guests arrived. I also wanted to have something that would go well with anything else I planned to serve, whether it was roasted fingerling potatoes or some crusty bread or charcuterie. This fit the bill.

The superstars of this fondue are the shiitake mushrooms and Roquefort cheese, two ingredients high in umami. The Roquefort in particular is super high in umami. It's an aged cheese, like Parmigiano-Reggiano. As we know, the longer a cheese ages, the more glutamates concentrate in it; the more glutamates, the more umami.

Use the best-quality cheese you can buy here. I prefer triple crème Brie over double crème because it's creamier when melted. Pick up a white wine that you would actually drink. The better the cheese and the better the wine, the better this fondue will be.

- 1½ teaspoons extra-virgin olive oil
- 4 ounces fresh shiitake mushrooms, stemmed and diced
- 1 teaspoon fresh thyme leaves
- 1 shallot, thinly sliced or minced
- 1 cup dry white wine, like Sauvignon Blanc or Pinot Gris, plus more if needed
- 12 ounces triple crème Brie, rind removed, cut into pieces, plus more if needed
- 2 ounces Roquefort, crumbled, plus more if needed

- 1 tablespoon all-purpose flour
- ½ teaspoon freshly ground black pepper
- 1 tablespoon black or white truffle butter (see Sources, page 248) or unsalted butter

. . . . . . . . . . . . . . .

**FOR DIPPING**

- 1 pound roasted shiitakes or mini yellow potatoes
- 1 baguette or loaf of sourdough bread
- Charcuterie, like salami or ham

*continued*

# Truffle Brothers

**A**ROUND THE TIME THAT Umami Burger opened was when I first met Michael and Marco Pietroiacovo, the Truffle Brothers. All the best restaurants knew them, and it was a full-on fiesta in the wintertime when the first white, then black, truffles were in season. I made ultra-luxe burgers with mounds of white truffles grated over them for special events.

If umami is the most satisfying of all the flavors, truffles are the most intoxicating of all umami flavors—the most intoxicating of all foods.

The Truffle Brothers have their own store in L.A. as well as a website (see Sources, page 248). All their products are umami flavor bombs: perfect cherry tomatoes in cans imported direct from Italy, anchovies and dried mushrooms, a large array of truffle products, and perfect cheeses. It's a paradise of goodness, and it's hard to be a bad chef when you cook with their stuff. Use the finest products, and with good technique and a great recipe you can make sublime food.

1. Heat the olive oil in a small skillet over medium heat. When the oil starts to smoke, throw in the shiitake mushrooms and sauté for 1 minute, then add the thyme and shallot. Turn the heat down to low.

2. While the mushrooms and shallot soften in the pan, place a fondue pot or small saucepan on the stove over medium-low heat and pour in the wine.

3. In a bowl, combine the Brie and Roquefort and sprinkle the flour over the cheeses. The flour will thicken the fondue as the cheeses melt.

4. When the wine just starts to simmer, add a big handful of the cheese mixture and whisk to combine. When the cheese has melted, throw in another big handful, then whisk again. Keep the pot at a bare simmer; if the heat's too high, the cheeses will separate.

5. Add the remaining cheese, as well as the pepper and butter.

6. When everything's nice and smooth, add the mushroom-shallot mixture, whisking constantly. If the fondue has a thinner consistency than you'd like, no big deal, just add a bit more Brie or Roquefort to taste. Conversely, if you think it's too thick, pour in a little more wine.

7. When the fondue hits the consistency you like, bring the fondue pot or saucepan, roasted vegetables, bread, and charcuterie out to the table for your guests. If you're using a fondue pot, set it over the flame to keep it warm; otherwise, the fondue will stay warm in the saucepan for 15 minutes or so. Return the pot to the stove to warm over low heat as necessary.

8. Serve the fondue with the rest of the wine, and if you have another bottle of white wine, bring that out, too.

**FLAVOR TIP**

Roquefort is a delicious but superstrong cheese. What's cool about this dish is that the Brie mellows it out and brings the dish into harmony.

# LAMB KEFTA

**SERVES 4 TO 6**

**K**EFTA IS A PREPARATION OF GROUND MEAT, SORT OF LIKE a ground-meat kabob. It's often made with ground lamb, and that's what I use here. But lamb doesn't have a whole lot of umami on its own, so I rely mostly on technique to bring out the umami. After marinating the ground lamb with *chermoula*, a thick North African sauce made with fresh herbs, ground spices, and lemon juice, I sear it on the grill to trigger the Maillard reaction, which then creates that delicious umami flavor. The kefta is then served with a rich almond sauce.

### CHERMOULA

- 1 cup chopped fresh flat-leaf parsley
- 1 cup chopped fresh cilantro leaves
- 4 garlic cloves, peeled
- 2 tablespoons fresh lemon juice
- 2 tablespoons olive oil
- 1 teaspoon paprika
- 1 teaspoon ground cumin
- ½ teaspoon ground coriander
- ¼ teaspoon cayenne pepper
- Pinch of Vadouvan (optional; page 42)

### LAMB

- 1½ pounds ground lamb shoulder or leg
- 1 medium onion, chopped
- 1½ teaspoons sea salt
- ½ teaspoon freshly ground black pepper
- Canola oil, for the grill

### FOR SERVING

- Pita bread (optional)
- 1 recipe Marcona Skordalia (recipe follows)
- ½ cup chopped fresh flat-leaf parsley

*continued*

1. **MAKE THE CHERMOULA:** Combine all the ingredients in a blender and puree until smooth.

2. **ADD THE LAMB:** With the chermoula still in the blender, add the ground lamb, onion, salt, and pepper. Blend until everything is well incorporated.

3. Using a spoon or a spatula, transfer the lamb mixture to a baking dish, pressing it down evenly. (You can use any size dish you have on hand. Just make sure to spread the mixture at least 2 inches thick, as you'll be cutting it into logs later.) Cover with plastic wrap and refrigerate for at least 2 hours, or make it a day ahead and keep it in the fridge overnight.

4. Preheat a grill to high and oil the grate with the canola oil.

5. Pull the lamb from the fridge and cut it into 4-by-1-inch rectangles.

6. When the grill is superhot, carefully add the lamb logs crosswise on the grates. You're looking for a hard sear on all four sides. I like grilling the lamb to medium-rare, 6 to 8 minutes total. If you're serving with pita bread, throw that on the grill now, too, until slightly charred on each side and warmed through.

7. To serve, spoon some Marcona Skordalia onto serving plates, then place 2 logs of kefta on top of each and some pita bread on the side, if you'd like. Garnish with a sprinkling of parsley on each plate.

# MARCONA SKORDALIA

MAKES ABOUT
1¼ CUPS

**S**KORDALIA **IS A RICH GREEK GARLIC SAUCE THAT I'VE** made even richer by mixing in Marcona almonds—Spanish almonds that have a softer, more velvety texture than California almonds. You can find them at Whole Foods and Trader Joe's, or order a bag on Amazon, but if you can't find them, you can use regular almonds instead. The sauce can be paired with the Lamb Kefta (page 188) and also goes well with roast beef.

- 1 small Yukon gold potato, peeled
- ½ cup extra-virgin olive oil
- 1 cup Marcona almonds
- ½ cup water
- 1 tablespoon chopped garlic
- Juice of ½ lemon
- Sea salt

1. Place the potato in a medium saucepan. Cover with cold water and bring to a boil over medium-high heat. Boil the potato until it's very soft, about 25 minutes.

2. Transfer the potato to a blender and add the olive oil, almonds, water, garlic, lemon juice, and a pinch of salt. Puree until very smooth.

3. Taste, then season with salt as needed.

4. It'll keep in the fridge for up to 3 days. It's great right out of the fridge, or warm it through before using.

SiDeS

**Y**OUR SIDES OF RICE AND VEGGIES DON'T have to be overshadowed by the main event. Strategically infuse them with umami flavors, and these will be just as sensational as everything else on your plate.

*Highlighted ingredients are staples of the Umami Pantry (page 24).*

# STEWED GIGANTE BEANS

**SERVES 6 TO 8**

**G**IGANTE BEANS ARE THE LARGE WHITE BEANS YOU OFTEN SEE IN Mediterranean cooking, and you can find them at Mediterranean groceries as well as stores like Whole Foods. They have a terrific creamy texture; they also absorb flavor exceptionally well, which makes them an ideal candidate for stews. In this recipe the Umami Ketchup gives the gigante beans an extra oomph of flavor, and the liquid from the Peppadew peppers cuts through with a lively brightness. The olive oil drizzle at the end highlights the tomato and pulls the whole dish together, so use the kind you keep tucked away for special occasions. Because this is definitely a special occasion. Soak the beans the night before.

Serve the beans with the Sweet and Savory Brisket (page 174) or Championship Chili (page 170).

- **1 pound dried gigante beans** (see headnote)
- **2 tablespoons tomato paste**
- **1 tablespoon of liquid from jarred Peppadew peppers** (optional; see page 248)
- **2 tablespoons Umami Ketchup** (page 35)
- **Sea salt and freshly ground black pepper**
- **Really great olive oil—the best you have**
- **Fresh chives, chopped** (optional)

1. The night before you plan to serve, place the beans in a large pot. Cover with water and let soak overnight.

2. The next day, drain the beans and refill the pot with water, just enough to cover. Bring the beans to a boil, then reduce to a simmer. Cook until the beans are super tender but not falling apart, 1½ to 2 hours.

3. When the beans are tender, reserve 2 tablespoons of the cooking water, then drain the beans.

4. Put the beans back on the stove over medium heat. Add the reserved cooking water, tomato paste, liquid from the Peppadews, if using, ketchup, and salt and pepper to taste. Mix everything together to combine. Bring the heat down to a gentle simmer and let the stew reduce until melded together and there's just a little liquid left in the pot, about 10 minutes. Just before serving, hit it with that really great olive oil and a sprinkling of chives, if desired.

5. Store any leftovers in an airtight container in the fridge. It'll be great tomorrow morning with eggs; beyond that it'll keep for up to 4 days.

# REFRiED BEANS

SERVES 6 TO 8

**R**EFRIED BEANS ARE too often too plain and boring. To get beans full of flavor and aromatics, all you need is a little bit of technique. These refried beans are literally exploding with umami from the caramelized onions, confit garlic, and Cotija cheese that's grated on top at the end.

For this recipe, I like using Rancho Gordo's heirloom pinto beans, which you can get on Amazon or, if you're buying in bulk, on Rancho Gordo's website, but most any dried beans will work. Whatever you do use, you won't need lard: Some chefs fry the beans in the fat, but I think it sometimes can mask the flavor of the beans. So I keep this one vegetarian all the way. In fact I think it actually has more flavor than most versions made with lard!

- 1 pound dried pinto beans
- Dried red pepper flakes (optional)
- 2 medium onions, peeled
- Sea salt and freshly ground black pepper
- 6 cloves Garlic Confit (page 38)
- 2 tablespoons really good olive oil
- Cotija cheese, for serving

1. The night before you plan to make this, place the pinto beans in a large pot. Cover with water and let soak overnight.

2. The next day, drain the beans and refill the pot with water, just enough to cover. Bring to a boil, then reduce to a simmer. Cook until the beans are super tender but not falling apart, 1½ to 2 hours; start checking them after an hour or so. If you want a hit of heat, throw in a pinch of dried red pepper. Don't salt the beans just yet—wait until the beans are drained and cooked so you can salt to taste.

3. While the beans cook, caramelize the onions (see page 41).

4. When the beans finish cooking, drain them over a bowl to reserve the liquid. Set the cooking liquid aside.

5. Carefully place the beans in a food processor and season with 1 teaspoon of salt and a few grinds of black pepper to taste. Add the caramelized onions and confit garlic. Puree until well blended and creamy. Taste again and adjust your seasonings. I like refried beans that have a thick consistency, but if you like yours a little looser, blend in the reserved bean liquid, ¼ cup at a time.

6. Fry the beans: In the same pan that you caramelized the onions, heat up the olive oil over medium heat. When the oil is hot, add the beans to the pan and sauté for about 2 minutes, or until the beans have softened into one mass. As they sauté, the beans will soak up the oil and its flavor, which is why you definitely want to use the good oil.

7. Finish with salt and pepper, then grate the cheese over the beans. Serve.

# CABBAGE "NORCINA"

SERVES 4 TO 6

**T**HIS DECADENT SIDE DISH IS BASED ON PASTA ALLA NORCINA, a dish with sausages and black truffles, usually in a cream sauce. I use cabbage here instead of pasta to turn this into a savory side that comes together very quickly. While the truffles are expensive, they are what make this dish; that said, you can still make a great version using just the truffle butter (available through Truffle Brothers, Amazon, or specialty grocery or cookware stores) or ordinary butter instead.

---

- Sea salt
- 2 sweet Italian sausages, cooked
- 1 tablespoon black truffle butter (see headnote) or unsalted butter
- 1 large green or Savoy cabbage (about 4 pounds), cored and thickly shredded
- 1 tablespoon freshly grated Parmigiano-Reggiano
- 1 teaspoon black truffle puree
- Freshly ground black pepper

1. Set a pot of salted water over high heat.

2. While you're waiting for the water to boil, remove the sausages from their casings, place the sausages in a food processor, and pulse just until crumbled. Melt the butter in a large skillet over medium-high heat, then add the crumbled sausage to the pan. Sauté for 5 minutes, until the meat starts to crisp. Set aside.

3. When the water has come to a boil, blanch the cabbage for 45 seconds. Drain well, running the cabbage under cold water to stop the cooking process.

4. Add the cabbage to the sausage. Stir for 2 minutes, until everything is incorporated well. Add the Parmesan, black truffle puree, and salt and pepper to taste. Serve.

# QUICK-COOKED JAPANESE-STYLE COLLARDS

**SERVES 4**

**M**OST FOLKS STEW COLLARDS FOR DAYS, AND I LOVE that preparation, but here's an alternative with miso and sake that takes just 5 minutes to make. This is excellent topped with Savory Sabayon (page 44).

- 1 pound collard greens
- 1 tablespoon white miso
- 1 tablespoon water
- 2 tablespoons canola oil
- 3 large garlic cloves, minced or pressed through a garlic press
- Drop of fish sauce (optional)
- ¼ cup plus 2 tablespoons sake or mirin

1. De-rib the collard greens by cutting the tough stems and ribs from the leaves. Roll the collards up tightly and slice into ribbons.

2. Mix the miso with the water to liquefy it.

3. Heat the oil in a large skillet or wok over medium heat. When it starts to ripple, add the garlic and cook, stirring, for 1 minute.

4. Add the collards to the pan and cook, stirring, for 30 seconds, then add the miso water and a drop of fish sauce, if you are not making these vegetarian.

5. When the water evaporates, deglaze the pan with the sake or mirin. Let the sake evaporate completely, 1 to 2 minutes. Serve.

**NOTE:**

You could make this vegetarian by omitting that drop of fish sauce.

# FRIED SWEET ONION STRINGS

**SERVES 2 TO 4**

**W**HEN YOU WANT A crunchy side for a rich main dish, these fried onion strings will do. I like the smoky spice kick that comes from the togarashi, the red Japanese spice powder that you can pick up at Asian markets or order on Amazon, but you can use cayenne pepper if that's what you have. Try the onion strings alongside Chicken Confit with Dirty Farro (page 158) or with a burger (pages 104 to 106).

- 2 cups buttermilk
- 1 teaspoon pimentón (smoked paprika)
- 1 Vidalia onion, peeled and halved
- Canola, vegetable, or peanut oil, for frying
- 1 cup all-purpose flour
- 1 cup cornmeal, medium grind
- ½ teaspoon togarashi or cayenne pepper
- Sea salt
- 1 tablespoon freshly ground black pepper

1. Pour the buttermilk in a large bowl and stir in the paprika.

2. With a mandoline placed over the bowl of buttermilk, carefully and thinly slice each half of the onion directly into the buttermilk. Using a spoon, or your hands if you don't mind getting messy, coat the onion well with the buttermilk. Place the bowl in the fridge and let marinate for an hour.

3. When the hour is almost up, get ready to deep-fry: Place a deep pot (preferably one that retains heat well, like a Dutch oven) on the stove and pour in 2 inches of frying oil. Place a food thermometer in the oil and heat over medium heat until the oil hits 400°F.

4. Meanwhile, mix the flour, cornmeal, togarashi or cayenne, 1 tablespoon of salt, and the pepper together in a large bowl. Place a baking sheet next to the stove, line it with a few paper towels, and place a rack on top. This is where you'll drain the onion strings once they're fried.

5. Take the onion out of the fridge and, using tongs, lift out some onion pieces. Shake off any excess buttermilk, then dredge the strings in the flour-cornmeal mixture. Carefully drop them into the oil.

6. Fry the onion strings until they're golden and crispy, 3 to 4 minutes. Remove to the rack to let drain. Season with a bit of salt. Repeat with the remaining onion in the buttermilk. Bring the oil temp back to 400°F between each batch.

7. Serve warm.

# MUSHROOM-LEEK CASSEROLE

**THIS IS A GREAT VEGETARIAN SIDE THAT FEA**tures layers of umami-packed mushrooms with leeks mixed in for a bit of sweetness. Shiitake, oyster, and porcini work best in this casserole, but use what you like.

- 3 pounds assorted fresh mushrooms, such as shiitake, oyster, and porcini, cleaned, trimmed, and sliced
- 1 pound sliced leeks, white and light green parts only, well washed
- Sea salt and freshly ground black pepper
- 2 tablespoons chopped fresh flat-leaf parsley
- 16 tablespoons (2 sticks) unsalted butter, cut into tablespoon-sized pieces
- 1 cup heavy cream
- 3 to 4 cups Parmesan Bread Crumbs (page 48), untoasted

1. Preheat the oven to 375°F.

2. Spread a quarter of the mushrooms and leeks to cover the bottom of a heavy 9-by-13-inch casserole dish. Season with salt, pepper, and a bit of parsley, then dot with 4 tablespoons of the butter and cover with ⅓ cup of the cream. Spread another quarter of the mushrooms and leeks on top, with another round of seasoning, 4 more tablespoons of butter, and another ⅓ cup of cream. Make another layer using a quarter of the mushrooms and leeks, followed by the seasoning, 4 tablespoons of butter, and the rest of the cream. For the fourth and final layer, spread with the remainder of the mushrooms and leeks, season, and top off with the last bits of butter.

3. Shower the top of the casserole with enough Parmesan Bread Crumbs to cover it, and bake until the mushrooms are nice and tender and the crust on top is golden brown, 20 to 30 minutes. Serve.

# PEAS WITH ROQUEFORT

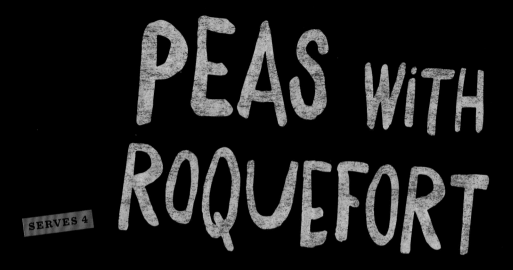

**A**S A KID, I DREADED PEAS. THEY WERE TOO OFTEN TASTELESS AND mushy, and I did all I could to avoid having to eat them. As an adult, though, I've learned to prepare them in a way that I love. Here, with aged blue cheese on top, this side dish pairs the young (peas) with the old (cheese) to great effect.

Take advantage of the sweetness of fresh English peas when they're in season. When they're not, frozen petite peas, which are younger, sweeter, and more tender than regular frozen peas, give excellent results. Buy the best quality you can find.

---

- 1 pound shelled fresh English peas or frozen petite peas
- 2 tablespoons unsalted butter
- 3 ounces Roquefort or Gorgonzola, crumbled
- Sea salt and freshly ground white pepper

1. First, steam the peas: Fill a pot with about an inch of water and set over high heat. When the water starts to boil, put the peas in a steamer basket, place it in the pot, and cover. The peas are done when they're tender, 4 to 5 minutes for fresh peas or 3 to 4 minutes for frozen petite peas.

2. Remove the steamer basket from the pot, drain the water, and place the peas in the pot. Add the butter and cheese and stir to melt. Season with salt and pepper to taste. Serve.

# CARAMELIZED ROOT VEGETABLES

**MAKES AS MUCH AS YOU'D LIKE**

CARAMELIZING VEGETABLES IS A GREAT TECHnique to bring umami to the fore. This dish will get you to your local farmers' market—the fresher the veggies, the better this will be.

It doesn't really matter what vegetables you use as long as they are dense and can take the heat (so no tomatoes or spinach). The more vegetables, the merrier!

## I LIKE TO USE

- Carrots, peeled
- Turnips, peeled
- Small onions or shallots, peeled
- Beets, peeled
- Brussels sprouts, cored with tough ends trimmed
- Parsnips, peeled
- Leeks, washed well, trimmed, green parts removed, then sliced in half lengthwise
- Fennel, cored
- Butternut squash, peeled, seeded, and cut into equal-sized cubes
- Fingerling potatoes, peeled or unpeeled, your choice
- Garlic cloves, peeled

## TO CARAMELIZE THE VEGETABLES

- Olive oil
- Sea salt and freshly ground black pepper
- Leaves from a bunch of thyme or a large pinch of herbes de Provence
- Fresh lime juice
- Pinch of Vadouvan (optional; page 42)

*continued*

1. Preheat the oven to 400°F.

2. While the oven preheats, prep the vegetables and cut them into similar sizes; leave whole any that are smaller than a golf ball.

3. In a large skillet, heat 1 tablespoon olive oil over medium heat. Working in batches if you have more vegetables than room in the pan, sauté the vegetables with a pinch of salt, pepper, and the thyme leaves or herbes de Provence until the vegetables have softened slightly. How long that will take will depend on the vegetables you're using; generally it takes just a few minutes per batch. Add a tablespoon of oil to the pan between batches.

4. Transfer the vegetables to a roasting dish or baking sheet where they won't crowd one another—they need a little bit of elbow room to caramelize properly. Drizzle them with more olive oil and roast in the oven, turning occasionally with a wide spatula, until they're well caramelized and tender when pierced, about 30 minutes.

5. Remove the vegetables from the oven and sprinkle with lime juice and the Vadouvan, if using. Taste and reseason if necessary. Serve warm.

# GRILLED RADICCHIO

**R**ADICCHIO CAN BE A LITTLE BITTER WHEN EATEN RAW. TO MELLOW it out, I like to throw it on the grill for a few minutes, dress it up with good balsamic vinegar, and finish it with garlic-infused oil. This is incredibly easy to make, especially if you already have the grill up and running.

Note: Radicchio often is available in both round and oblong shapes. I prefer the round-headed ones for grilling, as they are easier to cut into quarters. If you use oil from Garlic Confit, you can skip the second step of the recipe.

---

- ¼ cup oil from Garlic Confit (page 38) **or olive oil**
- 2 to 4 garlic cloves, minced, if not using oil from Garlic Confit
- 2 heads radicchio, preferably the round ones, cored and quartered
- ¼ cup balsamic vinegar
- Sea salt and freshly ground black pepper

1. Get your grill going on high heat.

2. If you are using oil from Garlic Confit, skip to the next step. If you are not: Place the plain olive oil in a saucepan with the minced garlic. Heat over low heat to cook the garlic slightly and infuse the oil with garlic flavor, just a few minutes.

3. Brush all sides of the quartered radicchio with some oil from Garlic Confit or the garlic-infused olive oil. Place the radicchio quarters on the hot grill and cook until they soften and you get some nice char marks on them, about 5 minutes, turning halfway through so they cook evenly.

4. Remove the radicchio to a platter and drizzle with the remaining garlic oil and the balsamic vinegar, and finish with some salt and pepper to taste. Serve.

# UMAMI'D RICE

**SERVES 4**

**T**HIS RICE IS PERFUMED WITH CHICKEN STOCK AND A little bit of Umami Master Dust, and is an easy way to perk up any meal. For an even more indulgent version, use the truffle rice from Truffle Brothers (see Sources, page 248).

- 1½ cups white rice, preferably medium-grain
- 3 cups chicken stock
- Pinch of Umami Master Dust (page 32)

Rinse the rice a few times, then place it in a large saucepan with the stock and a pinch of master dust. Bring to a boil uncovered, then immediately cover and turn the heat down to super low. Cook for 20 minutes. Turn off the heat and let the rice rest, covered, for 5 minutes. Fluff with a fork or chopsticks and serve.

# RiS-OAT-O

**T**RADITIONAL RISOTTO IS time consuming. It first involves a sauté and then adding stock one ladle at a time as you control the cooking exactly to the doneness you want. While this technique works with any pasta or rice, it also works with quick-cooking steel-cut oats, which I use in this umami-laden side that comes together in just a few minutes. If you have some leftover the next morning, it beats breakfast any day.

**SERVES 4**

- ½ onion, finely chopped or pureed
- 2 tablespoons olive oil
- 1 cup quick-cooking steel-cut oats
- 8 dried porcinis or any other dried wild mushrooms
- 3 cups chicken stock
- Pinch of saffron
- 1 tablespoon Umami Master Sauce (page 34)
- 1 tablespoon unsalted butter
- 1 teaspoon sherry vinegar

1. In a saucepan over low heat, cook the onion in the olive oil, stirring gently until soft and translucent. Add the oats and stir to coat, then add the dried mushrooms. Cook the oats and mushrooms until al dente and creamy, 5 to 7 minutes.

2. In a small saucepan, warm the chicken stock over medium-low heat until it simmers, then add the saffron and master sauce. Keep the stock at a low simmer.

3. Add a ladle of stock to the oats and cook, stirring, until the liquid is almost gone. Continue adding one ladle of stock at a time, stirring, and waiting for the liquid to nearly evaporate before adding the next ladle, 7 minutes total. During this time, the oats will soften.

4. As the 7-minute mark nears, start tasting for doneness. The oats should be soft, but al dente and definitely not mushy. When it's the consistency you like, turn off the heat and stir in the butter and vinegar. Let cool for a few minutes and serve.

# UMAMI'D FREGOLA SARDA

SERVES 6

**T**HIS RECIPE SHOWS HOW A LITTLE BIT OF UMAMI CAN transform even the simplest dish. The umami elements—fish sauce, soy sauce, sherry vinegar, and Parmesan cheese—are the neutral base for some riotous flavors.

Fregola sarda are little dense balls of semolina pasta, and they're pre-toasted for added flavor. Some recipes have you boil and drain them like noodles; I cook them like risotto here. The stock is the most important ingredient because it provides the basis for the umami flavor; in a pinch, you can turn a premade demi-glace, like the ones from Savory Choice, into a stock by diluting it with water to taste (I usually start with equal parts demi-glace and water and adjust from there). If you happen to have any leftover meat from a braise, add it at the end to make this a one-pot meal. This dish also goes well with Smoked Duck Breasts (page 155).

- 1 quart chicken stock, duck stock, demi-glace that has been diluted with water, or whatever stock you have on hand, preferably homemade
- 1 (17-ounce) package of toasted fregola sarda (see headnote)
- 1 tablespoon olive oil
- 1 garlic clove, minced
- Sea salt and freshly ground black pepper
- 1 tablespoon unsalted butter
- Dash of fish sauce
- Dash of good soy sauce
- Dash of Sriracha sauce
- Dash of sherry vinegar
- Braised meat, for serving (optional)
- Parmigiano-Reggiano, for grating
- Cubes of foie gras, for serving (optional)

1. Bring the stock to a simmer in a saucepan and keep it at a low simmer.

2. In another saucepan, sauté the fregola with the olive oil and garlic until fragrant, then add a ladle of stock and stir. When most of the stock has been absorbed, add two more ladles of stock and stir again. This process is like making risotto and you don't want to rush it—the flavors need time to develop. Keep adding stock, two ladles at a time, until you've added about three quarters of it. Add salt and pepper to taste.

3. When the fregola is softened, about 15 minutes, add the last of the stock, along with the butter and dashes of fish sauce, soy sauce, Sriracha, and sherry vinegar. Shake the pan until the fregola becomes glossy and almost all of the liquid has reduced to the consistency of a sauce. Pour onto a plate and tap the bottom of the plate on the counter so the fregola settles into one layer. If you're having this with braised meat, place that on top. Finish with a wisp of Parmesan.

4. For a more indulgent dinner-party version, sear a few small cubes of foie gras and sprinkle them on top, too.

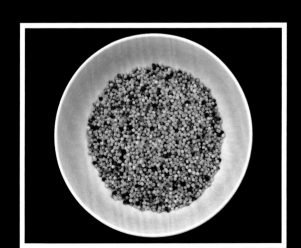

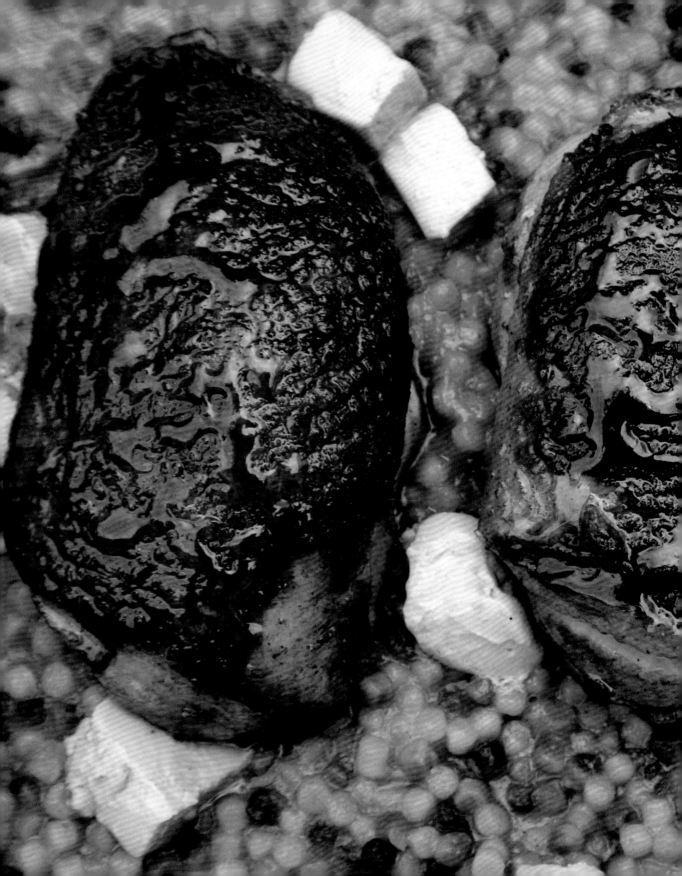

# Think You Hate It? Think Again

**TASTE IS MALLEABLE.** There was a time when I had a whole list of foods I wouldn't eat. Sweetbreads? Nope. Uni? No way. Didn't like sushi, either. But now I don't hesitate to order sweetbreads at a great Italian restaurant or splurge on a high-quality sushi dinner with a trusted chef as my guide.

The changes in my palate didn't happen overnight. It took a lot of proactive effort on my part over a long period of time to teach myself to enjoy these foods. And this is something you can do, too, with any food you think you hate. A number of studies have shown that we can indeed expand our palate to like—even love—a food or ingredient we once hated. In fact you've probably already done this: Think about the first time you tasted beer or coffee. Did you recoil from the bitterness? And despite that first impression, do you now like those drinks, even seek them out?

The key is repetition. In one study, even elementary school–aged kids learned to like vegetables such as carrots through repeated tastings. As an adult you probably came around to liking beer and coffee in part because you just continued to drink them and probably tasted a few different brew styles. Similarly for any food you hate now, keep trying it. Or try a preparation that changes the texture of the food. Ideally try it prepared in different ways at different restaurants. If you loathed steamed Brussels sprouts as a kid, try them roasted the next time they're on the menu at your neighborhood restaurant. You might hate chicken livers, as I did, but discover they're sublime when pureed into a mousse.

It might also help to pair foods you dislike with something you do like. If you hate mushrooms, sear a few slices and throw them in your favorite pasta sauce. Order a pizza with mushrooms along with another beloved topping. If you hate peas and love cheese, try them together, as in Peas with Roquefort (page 207).

Above all, have these transformative experiences with friends in happy settings. Positive associations off the plate can make the food taste better, too.

Your palate has memory, and you can expand that memory with new flavors. Stay open-minded and keep trying the things you think you hate, and you might be surprised at how little time it takes to turn hate into love.

# DRINKS
# AND
# DESSERTS

**T**O WIND DOWN OR TO TREAT YOURSELF, here are a few recipes to infuse your desserts and adult drinks with umami.

*Highlighted ingredients are staples of the Umami Pantry (page 24).*

# MEZCAL TRUFFLE COCKTAIL

**F**OR THIS COCKTAIL I USE TRUFFLE HONEY, which isn't overwhelming and accents the roasted, sweet agave flavor of the mezcal. The smoked sea salt around the rim of the glass adds a subtle depth to the drink and pulls it together. Most supermarkets carry smoked sea salt; if all else fails, you can order some from Amazon.

- **2 ounces high-quality mezcal** (I like El Silencio)

- **1 ounce Pineapple Syrup** (recipe follows)

- **¾ ounce fresh lime juice**

- **⅓ teaspoon truffle honey**

- **Smoked sea salt** (see headnote)

1. Place the mezcal in a cocktail shaker, along with the Pineapple Syrup, lime juice, and truffle honey. Fill the shaker about halfway with ice and shake.

2. Rim a glass with the smoked salt. Strain the shaker into the glass. Add an ice cube. Serve.

# PINEAPPLE SYRUP

**MAKES 1 CUP**

EVERY WELL-STOCKED BAR SHOULD INCLUDE A BOTTLE OR jar of simple syrup. This is just sugar dissolved in water, which is then blended or mixed with a spirit to make a cocktail. Here I infuse a simple syrup with fresh pineapple, which adds a tangy, tropical flavor to any cocktail you make. The pineapple sits in the syrup for two days, which might seem long, but it's necessary for full flavor.

- 1 cup sugar
- 1 cup water
- ½ cup peeled, cored, and cubed fresh pineapple

1. Combine the sugar and water in a small saucepan over medium heat. Bring it to a simmer and stir it a few times until the sugar has completely dissolved and the liquid is thick, a few minutes. Remove from the heat and set aside to cool.

2. When the syrup has cooled, place it in a jar with the pineapple. Shake and let sit in the fridge for 2 days. Strain (eat the pineapple) and use the syrup in cocktails.

3. Keep the syrup in the fridge, covered, where it will last for up to 1 month.

# Choosing Wines

**I AM A WINE GUY. IN FACT** wine is what got me interested in flavor in the first place, which led to my appreciation of umami. Choosing wine is a huge deal. I like crisp, high-acid whites (from Burgundy, Germany, and Austria) that complement the food, or earthy, medium-bodied reds (from Rhône and Italy) that don't pick a fight. Some reds, like Rhône, Italian, and Loire Cabernet Francs, have a hint of earthy, barnyard funk, which seems to be the vinous version of the fifth taste.

Test your pairings beforehand and make sure the wine is at the proper temperature. If you have a massive, aged wine, like a great Pomerol, just drink it by itself with no food, or with a bit of aged cheese and bread. And remember, some wines are just not food wines, so don't force a pairing if it doesn't work.

# On Ice

**I CE—OR, RATHER, GOOD** water to make good ice—is an important part of making cocktails. After all, a beautiful spirit aged eighteen years is ruined in two seconds if you add an ice cube made of water with impurities and off-tasting flavors (like tap water). For that reason, use high-alkaline water, which has a higher pH level and less acidity than tap water and can be found at Whole Foods, to make ice cubes. Good bottled waters like Fiji work, too.

Big ice cubes are ideal for drinks meant for sipping because they won't dilute the drinks as quickly as small ones. To make big ice cubes, you'll need a big–ice cube mold, which can be found for a few bucks online from websites like Amazon.

# BURNT MISO SCOTCH

**MAKES 1 COCKTAIL**

**T**HE BEST BARTENDER AND THE BEST CHEF IN THE WORLD are both in control of one thing: balance. In this great winter drink, the Scotch is a bit spicy, and the savory Burnt Miso, balanced with the truffle honey, will warm you up. Squeeze in a bit of lemon juice if you want, but don't omit the bitters: They're crucial to round out the drink.

- **1 teaspoon Burnt Miso** (page 47)
- **1½ ounces aged Scotch**
- **2 teaspoons (½ ounce) truffle honey**
- **2 dashes of whiskey bitters, like Angostura**
- **Lemon or fresh lemon juice** (optional)

Combine the miso, Scotch, truffle honey, and bitters in a cocktail shaker and shake. Strain and pour into a glass. Add a drop or two of water and an ice cube. If you find the cocktail too musky for your taste, cut a slice of lemon and squeeze a bit of juice into the cocktail.

# Creating a Cheese Plate

**A** SELECTION OF CHEESES, or just one great cheese, is important to any umami-filled meal. Make sure to serve cheese at full room temperature, which could require being out of storage for up to 4 hours. Cheese is served after the main course, and before (or instead of) dessert.

Some of my favorites are washed-rind goat's milk cheeses, which can attain the gooey perfection of cow's milk cheeses. I also like fresh sheep's milk ricotta, Comté, Manchego, and, of course, Parmigiano-Reggiano, which is as good alone as it is grated over pasta. It stands up to red wines, which often linger at the end of the meal. Most other cheeses pair better with white or rosé wines. Chablis is another favorite cheese-friendly wine.

When you're shopping for cheese, start by looking at the labels. Many countries, including Italy and France, certify high-quality cheeses that are produced in accordance to strict standards. For Italian cheese, that label is D.O.P. (which stands for *Denominazione di Origine Protetta*, or "Protected Designation of Origin"); in France it's A.O.P., or *Appellation d'Origine Protégée* (which replaced the previous designation, A.O.C., *Appellation d'Origine Contrôlée*, or "Controlled Designation of Origin"). If you are attempting a cheese plate, have a cheesemonger sell you a progression of cheeses from goat's milk to sheep's milk to cow's milk, ending with the strongest blue cheeses. When serving, place them in the appropriate order as well.

# STRAWBERRIES AND BALSAMICO

**S**TRAWBERRIES AND BALSAMIC VINEGAR are great together, but to really elevate the combo, I use aged balsamic because it's already reduced over time into a syrup. Aging also brings out the umami-ness. Use the best aged balsamic vinegar that you can. It'll be worth the investment.

- ½ cup sugar
- ½ cup water
- 2 tablespoons honey
- ½ cup aged balsamic vinegar
- 3 pounds strawberries, hulled and sliced into quarters
- 8 scoops crème fraîche, vanilla gelato, or ice cream
- 1 teaspoon finely grated lemon zest

1. In a small, heavy saucepan over medium-high heat, combine the sugar, water, and honey and bring to a boil, stirring until the sugar dissolves. At that point, kill the heat and drizzle in the balsamic. This is going to be the syrup for the berries.

2. Place the strawberries in a large bowl. Pour the still-warm syrup over them and stir carefully, just enough so that each berry gets a good amount of syrup. Divide the strawberries and the syrup among eight bowls or dessert cups, followed by the crème fraîche, gelato, or ice cream. Sprinkle the lemon zest on top and serve quickly, before it melts.

# CHOCOLATE-TRUFFLE GANACHE

**C**HOCOLATE DOESN'T CONTAIN ANY GLUTAMATES, BUT I CONSIDER IT an honorary umami ingredient because it gives you the same full-palate-satisfying experience you get with other glutamate-rich ingredients. And this chocolate-truffle dessert definitely gives you that rush.

And yes, the recipe name is a play on words. The texture here is a bit like the filling you find inside chocolate truffle balls, but this ganache uses actual truffles, in the form of truffle honey and truffle salt. There's just enough of the honey and salt to call out the umami. The success of this recipe really relies heavily on the chocolate, so go with a high-quality, trusted producer (see page 24), like Scharffen Berger, Guittard, Callebaut, Valrhona, or Michel Cluizel. When it all comes together, this is one of the best desserts any chocolate lover will ever eat, and it comes together in all of 5 minutes.

Note: Vanilla paste is a paste made from the beans of vanilla pods; you can find it at specialty stores like Sur La Table and Williams-Sonoma, or online at Amazon.

- 1 cup heavy cream
- ¼ cup plus 2 tablespoons whole milk
- 1 large egg
- ¼ teaspoon instant espresso
- ¼ teaspoon vanilla paste (see headnote) or ½ teaspoon vanilla extract
- ½ teaspoon truffle honey
- 7 ounces good-quality 70 to 90% dark chocolate, chopped into small pieces
- Truffle salt
- Whipped cream, for serving (optional)

1. In a small saucepan over medium heat, heat the cream and milk. Whisk the egg in a medium bowl.

2. As the cream mixture comes to a boil, add the instant espresso, vanilla paste or extract, and truffle honey (see Flavor Tip).

3. As soon as the cream mixture boils, pull it off the heat. Carefully whisk a little bit of it into the bowl with the egg; if you add the hot liquid all at once, the egg will cook instead of staying liquid.

*continued*

4. Continue adding the cream mixture to the egg a bit at a time, still whisking, until you've added it all. Add the chocolate and stir until thoroughly combined. The chocolate will melt quickly, and the mixture will thicken.

5. Divide the ganache equally among four martini glasses or your choice of glassware. Cover loosely and place in the fridge. Let it set for 1 to 2 hours.

6. Before serving, finish with a sprinkle of truffle salt on top, then tap the bottom of the glass a few times for an even layer of salt. If you wish, serve with whipped cream.

## FLAVOR TIP

The instant espresso and vanilla function as flavor counterpoints, which I like to have when working with chocolate. Feel free to sub in other flavors, like ground hazelnuts or grated lemon or orange zest, by stirring them into the cream as it comes to a boil—don't forget to strain them out. The truffle is the star here, though (along with the dark chocolate notes).

# CHOCO-BANANA MEGA-CREPE

**SERVES 2**

**C**HOCOLATE, MY FAVORITE NON-UMAMI umami ingredient, satisfies in every way in this dessert crepe. Based on clafoutis, a fancy-named dessert that really is nothing more than a puffy crepe, it makes a great communal dessert at your next dinner party.

You could also replace the chocolate with dulce de leche for a banoffee pie version.

### BATTER

- ½ cup all-purpose flour
- ⅓ cup plus 2 tablespoons sugar
- ¼ teaspoon ground cinnamon
- Pinch of sea salt
- 1 cup half-and-half
- 3 large eggs, plus 1 large egg yolk

### BANANAS

- 2 ripe bananas, sliced
- 1 tablespoon unsalted butter
- 1 teaspoon sugar
- Splash of rum

### CHOCOLATE GANACHE

- 4 ounces good-quality 70% dark chocolate, chopped into small pieces
- ½ cup heavy cream

*continued*

blended. Cover the bowl with plastic wrap and place it in the fridge while you prepare the bananas.

4. **MAKE THE BANANAS:** In a cast-iron skillet over medium heat, sauté the banana slices with the butter and sugar until they're soft but not falling apart, about 2 minutes. Splash in the rum, wait a few seconds, and—being careful not to burn yourself—tilt the pan toward you. With a long match or lighter held over the pan, ignite to flambé the bananas. Turn off the heat, remove the bananas and set them aside, pour the crepe batter into the pan, and place the pan in the oven. Bake until the crepe is firm, 12 to 15 minutes.

5. **MEANWHILE, MAKE THE GANACHE:** Place the chocolate and cream in a small saucepan over low heat. Melt the chocolate into the cream, give it a good stir, and let it cool.

6. When the crepe is done, remove it from the oven. Top it with the bananas, drizzle it liberally with the ganache, fold it in half, cut it into wedges, and serve.

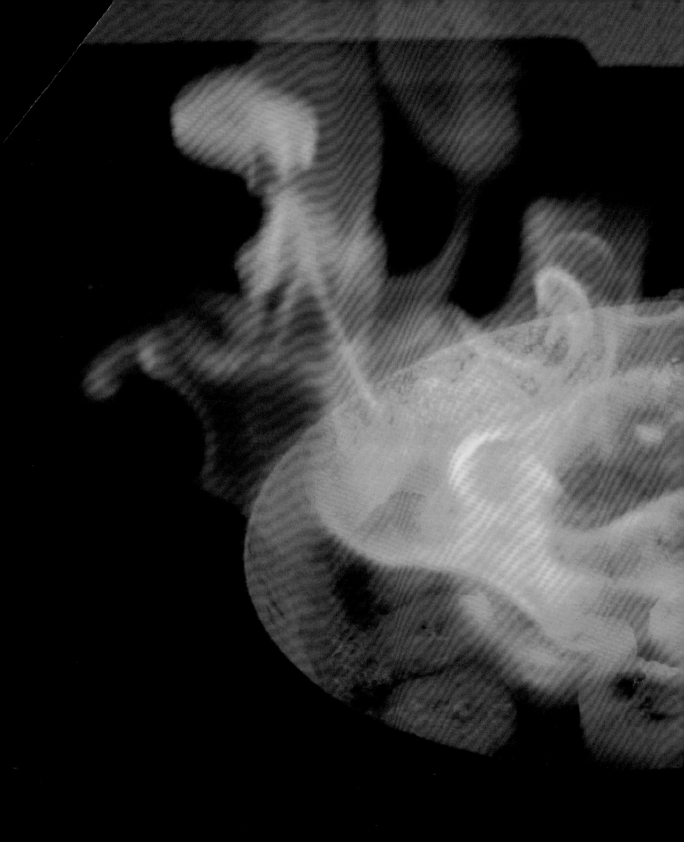

# MATCHA MAGIC CAKE

**M**ATCHA IS ONE OF THE ONLY UMAMI INGREDIENTS with a hint of sweetness to it, so I use it to make magic cake. This simple batter bakes into three separate layers: The bottom layer will be chewy and dense, the middle will have a custard-like texture, and the top layer will be spongy and airy. Magic!

Feel free to increase or decrease the matcha by ½ tablespoon or so to suit your personal preference.

- Nonstick cooking spray or butter, for the pan
- 4 large eggs, separated
- 3 drops of white vinegar
- 1 cup all-purpose flour
- 1½ tablespoons cooking-grade matcha
- 1½ cups confectioners' sugar
- 8 tablespoons (1 stick) unsalted butter, melted
- 1 tablespoon water
- 2 cups whole milk

**FOR SERVING**

- Confectioners' sugar
- Fresh berries

1. Preheat the oven to 325°F, with a rack in the middle.

2. Spray or butter an 8-inch nonstick square pan and set aside. If you don't have a nonstick pan, butter the pan and line it with parchment paper to prevent the cake from sticking.

3. In a large bowl with a hand mixer, beat the egg whites briefly, until they just start to foam, then add the white vinegar to stabilize them. Continue beating until very stiff peaks form. Set aside.

4. In a small bowl, sift the flour and matcha together.

*continued*

5. In another large bowl, whisk the egg yolks and the sugar until light in color, about 3 minutes. Still mixing, slowly add the butter. Add the water and beat again until everything is well combined.

6. Mix a little bit of the flour-matcha mixture into the yolks. Continue whisking it in a little at a time until it's fully incorporated.

7. Slowly stir the milk into the batter. At this point the batter will have a very thin, liquid consistency, similar to a very loose pancake batter. You might think this won't bake properly, but trust me, it will!

8. Carefully fold in the egg whites, one third at a time, until incorporated. These whites are key: They'll give the top layer of the cake a spongy, soufflé-ish quality.

9. Pour the batter into the cake pan and bake for 40 to 50 minutes, until the top is golden and the middle of the cake wobbles a little like Jell-O or crème brûlée when you shake the pan. Do not overbake.

10. Leave the cake in the pan to cool to room temperature. Run a knife around the sides of the cake, invert a plate over the pan, then, pressing the two together, invert the cake onto the plate. Remove the parchment, if using, then put a serving plate over the cake, invert again, and dust with confectioners' sugar. Serve with fresh berries.

**T MIGHT SOUND ODD, BUT TRUST ME: PRIZED** dried porcini mushrooms make this sweet dessert more earthy and complex. It's even a great dessert for those who don't think they like mushrooms—my kids scarfed it and didn't detect any mushroom flavor. This dessert, by the way, takes its name from the mushrooms themselves: *Porcini* is Italian for "piglet." You can buy porcini powder on Amazon, or blitz your own in a food processor or coffee grinder.

## CRUST

- 1 cup chocolate graham cracker crumbs
- 2 tablespoons sugar
- 1 tablespoon ground dried porcini mushrooms
- ½ teaspoon sea salt
- 8 tablespoons (1 stick) unsalted butter, melted

## FILLING

- 9 ounces bittersweet chocolate (65 to 75%), the best you can afford, chopped into small pieces
- 1 cup heavy cream
- 8 tablespoons (1 stick) unsalted butter, cut into pieces
- 2 large eggs, lightly beaten
- Splash of vanilla extract
- Splash of dark rum
- Pinch of sea salt

## CARAMEL

- ¼ cup sugar
- 2 tablespoons water
- 1 tablespoon ground dried porcini mushrooms

*continued*

1. Preheat the oven to 325°F, with a rack positioned in the middle.

2. MAKE THE CRUST: Throw the chocolate graham crumbs, sugar, ground dried porcinis, and salt into a food processor and pulse a few times to incorporate. Add the melted butter and pulse again until the mixture comes together. Press the mixture into a 9-inch tart pan with a removable bottom, cool in the freezer for 10 minutes, then bake for 10 minutes to firm up. Set it aside to cool while you make the filling.

3. MAKE THE FILLING: In a saucepan over low heat, melt the chocolate into the cream. Whisk in the butter, then the eggs, then the vanilla and rum. Season with the salt and whisk to emulsify. Take the pan off the heat.

4. Pour the chocolate filling into the crust. Return it to the oven and bake until it's completely set, about 15 minutes.

5. Remove to a cooling rack. Let cool completely.

6. MAKE THE CARAMEL: In a small saucepan over low heat, combine the sugar and water. Stir to dissolve the sugar, and increase the heat to medium. Once the mixture starts to boil, stop stirring and let it start to brown. At that point, occasionally shake the pan until it's uniformly caramelized and medium brown in color. Add the porcinis and stir. Let cool for 1 minute.

7. Pour the caramel over the cooled tart, leaving 1 inch of space around the edge. Remove the tart pan ring, slice the tart, and serve. Save the leftovers—if you have any—in the fridge for up to 1 day.

# Flavor Beyond Taste

T'S NOT JUST INGREDIENTS and technique that affect what you taste. Psychology plays a huge role, too: Color, for example, can impact the perception of flavor. In a study published in 2012 in the *Journal of Sensory Studies*, researchers had participants compare hot chocolate served in orange, cream, red, and white mugs. It was the same drink, but they rated the hot chocolate in the orange- and cream-colored mugs as tastier than the hot chocolate served in the red- and white-colored mugs. Or consider the heavy plates at some restaurants. A few studies, including one from Oxford University researcher Charles Spence, have shown that people think food is more enjoyable when it's served on a heavy plate and with heavy cutlery, as if we project the value of the plate onto the food itself.

Ambient sounds in your environment, even the pitch of the background music playing in the restaurant, affect how you taste. Spence and other researchers have found that some foods, like chocolate and beer, seem to taste sweeter if we eat or drink them while listening to high-pitched music, while low-pitched music brings out their bitterness. And in environments where the decibel level is super high, like in an airplane, Cornell University researchers found that our perception of umami flavors is enhanced while that of sweet flavors is somewhat suppressed. This might be one reason why people enjoy tomato juice on a noisy plane when they might not otherwise drink it on the ground.

Listening to sounds associated with the food you're eating can increase flavor intensity—think about how much better grilled meat tastes when you're outside, at a picnic, hearing it sizzle, compared to eating that same plate at home, in your dining room, no grill.

Chef Heston Blumenthal uses these ideas at his restaurants. At The Fat Duck he serves a dish with an iPod tucked into a conch. You put on the earbuds and listen to seagulls and other ocean sounds as you feast on seafood.

At home, experiment with sound and taste: Sip an ale or nibble on dark chocolate while listening to tracks heavy on the flutes. Then switch to something with more bass, and see if you taste the food differently. And when you prep for your next dinner party, let the food guide your playlist. Pull together tracks that will not only match the overall mood you're going for but will complement each course of your menu, too.

# SOURCES

THE INGREDIENTS IN THE BOOK CAN BE FOUND AT YOUR local supermarket, specialty grocer, or Asian grocery store. Sourcing tips for a few of the items follow.

### CALABRIAN CHILIES

Find jars of Calabrian chilies packed in oil at your local Italian deli or market, or at specialty shops like Williams-Sonoma and Sur La Table. You also can order it on Amazon.

### DRIED ANCHOVIES

Dried anchovies come in various sizes and can be found in Asian markets and sometimes in the Asian aisle of major American supermarkets. You can also find dried anchovies on Amazon.

### DUCK CONFIT

Look for duck confit at your local specialty grocer or butcher; you can also find it at Whole Foods, and even Costco sometimes carries it. Duck confit also can be ordered from dartagnan.com and Amazon.

### FAR WEST FUNGI

I love Far West Fungi for their dried mushrooms. They set up at various farmers' markets all over the San Francisco Bay Area, and their products are available online as well, at farwestfungi.com.

### MITSUWA MARKETPLACE

Mitsuwa is my go-to Japanese grocery store that carries pretty much everything you need in this book, including dried mushrooms, kombu, miso, yuzu kosho, and togarashi. There are a few locations in Los Angeles as well as several others in California. They also have stores in Chicago, Hawaii, New Jersey, and Texas. mitsuwa.com

### PEPPADEW PEPPERS

If you can't find Peppadews at your local grocery store, you can order jars online on Amazon. You can find more information about Peppadews at the website peppadewusa.com.

### POWDERED SOY SAUCE

Powdered soy sauce is available on Amazon.

### RANCHO GORDO

Rancho Gordo's heirloom beans are the best. You can find their beans on Amazon; you also can order beans directly from Rancho Gordo, at ranchogordo.com, though note that there is a shipping charge for orders less than $75.

### RED BOAT FISH SAUCE

You can find Red Boat in several sizes at Whole Foods, and many Asian grocery stores are starting to carry it, too. Or you can order it direct on redboatfishsauce.com.

### RUSTICHELLA D'ABRUZZO

Your local Italian deli, Whole Foods, or other specialty grocery store might carry Rustichella d'Abruzzo, my favorite brand of dried Italian pasta. You can also order it on Amazon.

### SAVORY CHOICE

For demi-glaces that are handy to keep in your pantry, Savory Choice is great and can be ordered from savorychoice.com.

### SHIO KOJI

Shio koji can be found in Japanese grocery stores; it'll often be packaged in a small pouch or jar. If you don't have a Japanese market near you, you can order it from Amazon.

### TRUFFLE BROTHERS

For truffles, truffle flour, truffle honey, truffle puree, truffle salt, truffle butter, truffle everything. Find them online at trufflebrothers.com.

### . . . AND IF ALL ELSE FAILS: AMAZON.COM

Amazon has everything you need to cook from this book, with some items sold in bulk so you can stock up. In addition to being a solid source for ingredients, Amazon offers great cooking equipment, too.

### ADDITIONAL READING ON UMAMI

The world of umami is vast, and researchers are discovering fascinating new stuff about it every day. The Umami Information Center, umamiinfo.com, is a great resource.

# INDEX

**Note:** Page references in *italics* indicate photographs.